Researching Architecture

2 Laboratorium

A series of volumes published by:
Hochschule Luzern – Technik & Architektur
Tina Unruh, CC Material, Struktur & Energie in Architektur

Researching Architecture

Andri Gerber, Tina Unruh, Dieter Geissbühler

Quart Publishers Lucerne

Researching Architecture
Volume 2 of the series Laboratorium

Editor: Hochschule Luzern – Technik & Architektur,
Tina Unruh, Competence Centre Material, Structure & Energy in
Architecture
Contributions by: Andri Gerber, Tina Unruh, Dieter Geissbühler
Design concept for the process presentations: C2F·Cybu Richli &
Fabienne Burri, Lucerne
English translation: Benjamin Liebelt, Berlin
Illustration editing: Dominique Neyerlin, Markus Henggeler
Graphic Design: Quart Publishers, Lucerne
Lithos: Printeria, Lucerne
Printing: Engelberger Druck AG, Stans

Original edition 2010: German (ISBN 978-3-03761-019-0)

Quart Publishers Ltd.
Denkmalstrasse 2, CH-6006 Lucerne
books@quart.ch, www.quart.ch

Printed in Switzerland

We are grateful for the Architecture Department's kind support
Hochschule Luzern – Technik & Architektur

Foreword

This publication dares to tread new paths. The authors venture into a jungle of disorientation and move from the question of research to ultimately asking how to develop a good building. The circular diagram they present deciphers the interacting parameters involved in the creative process of architecture.

An enormous forest of interpretation exists today. There have never been so many ways of choosing an architectural path. Like a GPS navigator, the tools presented in this book can be used to establish a clearance in that jungle. However here and there at the edge of the clearance, its perfect form is already being encroached upon, a result of the accelerating speed of our times that oppose the constant values of architecture. The only way out leads through one's own action, reflection and the experience gained from it, all of which is founded upon cultural roots and supported by scientific work. This book also addresses those aspects.

What remains is architecture that is – in its best sense – relative.

Lucerne, spring 2010, Ursula Stücheli
Architect, Lecturer HSLU – Technik & Architektur

Experimental Order
Architecture as research – a thesis

Is architecture research? Architects have addressed this question at regular intervals and continue to do so today.[1] There are many reasons for the current interest in the subject. The field in which architects work is becoming ever more complex and obscure. In recent years, a perception of architecture as research has developed, not least as an attempt to adapt to the changing environment. Such a consciousness of regarding the work as more than simply applying rules and fulfilling norms has not only developed among architects themselves. A large proportion of their work is based on seeking and researching the underlying conditions and requirements for design and construction, with the aim of understanding it better. Like other periods in history, the last two decades were influenced by a scientific revolution – new computer technologies for design and production – for architecture. The parametric planning and production technologies associated with them create a quantifiable design process. At first glance at least, the process of design therefore shifts from the apparently arbitrary nature of the creative act towards a "scientific" process. At the same time, the perception of research is also changing in other fields, in which a purely rational approach is relativised. So architecture seems to be moving closer to the natural sciences.

Growing interest in research in architecture is reflected in the large number of conferences and publications addressing the subject. Often, the focus lies on distinguishing between research *through* and research *on* architecture. Fields such as natural and human sciences, for instance construction physics and the history of architecture, are especially active in research on architecture.

Going beyond that distinction, this study attempts to address the question of research in architecture on a wider scale. The aim is to study the entire process of architectural production, which can only be described as research in its entirety. The intention is to determine the underlying conditions and requirements that make up

[1] For the former universities of applied science in Switzerland, the question of research became increasingly relevant as a result of the Bologna Process and the research responsibilities it entails. ("The universities of applied science carry out application-oriented research and development and thereby ensure the connection between science and practice. They integrate the results into teaching." Extract from Federal Law on Universities of Applied Science (Bundesgesetz über die Fachhochschulen, 1995)

the research aspect of architecture. The second part of this book records a wide range of approaches and studies the diversity of such research. As a result of theoretical studies, the requirements for regarding architecture as research are assessed using case studies in the third part of the book. A series of so-called preparations – which refer to the CVs of individual architects – is used to study what knowledge flows into the creative process of architecture and what knowledge is generated in that framework. Only by generating conclusions, from which the above-mentioned spatial knowledge can spring, does an architectural process also become a specific type of research.

The central instrument of the study is a circular diagram that illustrates how conclusions and knowledge are handled during the design process. It should not only improve the understanding of processes in architecture, but also serve as an impetus to reflect upon one's own work.

The origin of this study lies in a research project on the subject of *Architecture as Research*, which was carried out at the Lucerne Universtiy of Applied Science between the summer of 2008 and the autumn of 2009. The assumption at the start of the project was a discussion on architecture in the overlap between art and science, between *mythos* and *logos*. This working thesis was later relativised, since the discussion with Michael Hampe and Reto Geiser, which is included in the appendix of this publication, revealed that one should rather focus on the unique characteristics of architecture, its creative process and the knowledge derived from it, instead of deriving a definition of architecture from art and science. As a result, the study released itself from the initial thesis as work progressed and developed towards a perception of architecture as an independent form of knowledge.[2] The autonomous field of science, which is the result of the process of architectural work and the research it entails, is described here as spatial science. The term refers to the fact that it is a specific form of knowledge based on architecture that distinguishes itself from other forms of knowledge. Only a research process that is inherent in architectural work allows architectural science to be communicated and sustained. The knowledge inherent in the projects and constructed architecture

[2] Forms of knowledge are not discussed further here. In this respect, see Steffen Siegel, *Figuren der Ordnung um 1600*, Köln: Böhlau, 2009

are thereby not the same as the pure experiences of the architect. It is described as *spatial knowledge* since the architectural knowledge unfolds in planning the project and implementing space.

The project *Architecture as Research* is not intended to make architectural work scientific, objective or schematic. Instead, the authors aimed to better understand the processes and interrelations and clarify when and why architecture is a form of research. This study and the accompanying publication would not have been possible without the support of University of Lucerne, the Sub-Department of Technology and Architecture, and the Department of Architecture, for which the authors are grateful, as well as for the ability to participate in various conferences that enabled the constant exchange of ideas and a necessary questioning of the thesis. It provided the University of Lucerne with an important basis for applied research in architecture.

The illustrations in the text were produced using sketches by the five architects studied here. They are deliberately abstracted diagrams that illustrate themes such as space and technology. They are part of the project and can – albeit on a more abstract level as diagrams – also stimulate reflection on one's own work.

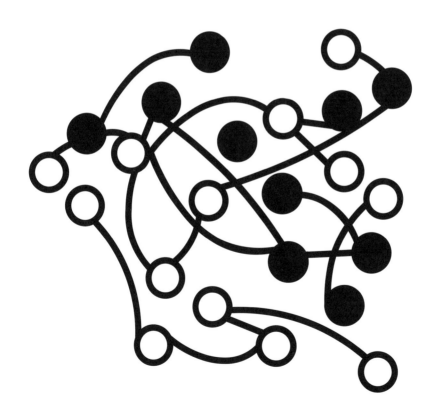

Biodiversity
Observations on scientific research

It is clearly more difficult to concede that the search for something different is the search for different forms of knowledge, rather than the search for another science.
Gernot Böhme[1]

Despite the field's own independence, discourse on research in architecture entails cognition of underlying principles of scientific research. This study does not use the standard perception of research for this purpose, instead focusing on deviations and relativisation at its fringes. Only by analysing what is meant by architecture as research can one name similarities with and differences from conventional, scientific research. The opening Böhme quotation applies in general: The aim is not to prove the scientific nature of architecture itself, but to discuss its specific knowledge and form as one of many types of knowledge, as well as identifying the processes of gathering cognition that lead to it.

Scientific research is methodical and systematic. It is a "planned, ordered approach with the aim of gaining new cognition and new knowledge, as well as solving practical problems."[2] It can be communicated and tested. Methodically, a distinction is made between deduction (top-down method) and induction (bottom-up method). There is also a third category developed by Charles Sanders Peirce, which is based on Aristotle – abduction, which describes a process in which an explanatory hypothesis is developed.[3]

Research always means gained cognition. Testable and communicable cognition means knowledge. A central problem of research and cognition is the "subject-object problem"[4] and the inherent different interpretations of research as "questioning" and "carefully seeking". To what extent does research describe the object or does it allow itself to be defined by the object? In standard scientific research, the subject and object remain separate. The researcher observes the object from a detached perspective. However in so-called

[1] Böhme 1980, p. 14
[2] Balzert, Schäfer, Schröder, Kern 2008, p. 6
[3] Peirce, Charles Sanders, 1974–1979, p. 106
[4] "Der für den Begriff der E. konstitutive Zusammenhang zwischen den (strukturierenden) Leistungen des E.subjekts und den Gegebenheiten des E.objekts bildet historisch gesehen das sogenannte Subjekt-Objekt-Problem. Die Explikation des Begriffs der E. in diesen und anderen Hinsichten erfolgt in der Erkenntnistheorie." "Erkenntnis" in: Mittelstrass 1980–1996, p. 375

[5] Nischik, Traude-Marie "'Forscher', Eine etymologische Studie, unter Berücksichtigung von Konrad von Megenbergs 'Buch der Natur'", in: Diemer 1978, p. 2

[6] Mittelstrass 1980–1996

[7] "Forschung", in: Mittelstrass 1980–1996, p. 533

[8] "Forschen Vb. 'Erkenntnis suchen, erkunden'. Das nur im Dt. (ursprünglich Hd.) bezeugte ahd. *forscon* (8 Jh.) mhd. *vorschen* 'erfragen, erforschen' ist vergleichbar mit lat. *poscere* 'fördern, verlangen, forschen, fragen' und aind. *prcchati* 'fragt'." Kluge 1989, p. 367

[9] "Forschung", *Enzyklopädie der Neuzeit*, Stuttgart/Weimar Verlag J. B. Metzler, p. 1057

[10] "Forschung", Enzyklopädie der Neuzeit, Stuttgart/Weimar Verlag J. B. Metzler, p. 1056

[11] "In der Vorrede zur zweiten Auflage der 'Kritik der reinen Vernunft' verweist Kant auf den Beginn der (empirischen) Naturwissenschaften. Mit den Entdeckungen Galileis, Torricellis und Stahls 'ging allen Naturforschern ein Licht auf. Sie begriffen, dass die Vernunft nur das einsieht, was sie selbst nach ihrem Entwurfe hervorbringt, dass sie mit Prinzipien ihrer Urteile nach beständigen Gesetzen vorangehen und die Natur nöthigen müsse auf ihre Fragen zu antworten [...]'. Mit der Begründung wissenschaftlicher Naturbetrachtung durch die Gesetze der Vernunft ist die – mit ihrer Hilfe konstruierte – Bestätigung im Experiment gekoppelt, das den Wissenschaftler zum 'Richter' der Natur erhebt. Sein Wirkungsfeld ist nicht auf die nachvollziehende Beobachtung des 'Schülers' beschränkt, sondern vielmehr durch vernunftversprechende, planvoll gelenkte Eigenerfahrung begrenzt. Vor allem im Hinblick auf das zweite Bestimmungselement kann daher – unabhängig von der Übernahme des Kant'schen Natur- und Wissenschaftsbegriffes –, Forschung als anerkannte Form positiver wissenschaftlicher Arbeit' angesehen werden." Nischik, Traude-Marie, in: Diemer 1978, p. 1–2

"sensual research", a connection is posited between the subject and object.[5]

Intuitive, sensual research is harder to define than more rational, traceable research. Both forms of research generate direct cognition regardless of their structural difference. Rational research also provides cognition into in-sight itself, which is defined as a "meta-competence of the second degree."[6] In other words scientific research must also reflect on research itself and must reflect its processes, as well as being able to communicate them.[7] So the result of research is cognition, which leads to knowledge. Knowledge can also be created by experience, which leads us to the "problem" of architecture, since its knowledge is based both on research and experience.

Contemporary understanding of scientific research only inadequately takes into account the fact that both the term and today's perception of it are historical constructs. Both have changed through time and will continue to do so. A look at the etymological roots of the key German terms *Forschung* (research) and *Erkenntnis* (cognition) is revealing. The term "Forschen" stems from the Middle High German "vorschen", which means to question or investigate and can be compared to the Latin *poscere* – to request, demand, to invoke, to inquire.[8] It was originally used both in legal and theological contexts. Corresponding terms in other languages were the French *recherche* – which appeared in the 17th Century – and the English term *research*, which is also very present in German today and only appeared in the 19th Century.[9] Until the middle of the 18th Century, the term *Forschung* was almost exclusively used in the plural form ("Forschungen") and "specifically denoted the collection of empirical data (and) only then transformed – in a similar way to history or progress – into a singularly used, pathos-laden synonym for cognition in general, thereby assuming the same meaning as science (knowledge and knowledge ideals)."[10]

The transformation of the term and its meaning is connected with its importance and increasing professionalisation, which led to consistent specialisation into fields. Decisive motors in this process were both empiricism and the theories of Immanuel Kant. He placed an emphasis on ratio, which he believed would produce a "new type of human, the researcher," and could be used to reject empiricism.[11]

Erkenntnis can also be traced back to a legal origin.[12] Basically the question of cognition and its limits is one of the "most debated subjects of modern philosophy. It arose in the context of the intellectual crises that have shaken Europe since the early 16th Century."[13]

Like the history of research, the history of cognition is characterised by a constant development towards rationalism and a rejection of everything sensual. This linear development towards Enlightenment and Kant is above all characterised by an emancipation of knowledge from faith.

The duality between empiricism and rationalism is of central importance in the development and transformation of the term research. Rationalism had its origins with Descartes, who "made mathematical cognition a model of the only possible form of cognition."[14] By contrast, empiricism stresses "the importance of experience for cognition. Thus the "origin of cognition [...] according to a rationalist approach is thought, while an empiricist [perceives] it predominantly in the senses."[15]

Empiricism uses the senses to approach the research object, while rationalism only uses reason. Since the time of Kant if not before, scientific research has been based on rationalism, with all else regarded as unscientific.

Alternative scientific models

This rational model was, not least due to its overwhelming dominance, never completely undisputed. Its general application has been increasingly questioned, especially in the last 50 years. An emphasis on the role of creativity and aleatory momentum developed, as well as an increasing awareness that science does not describe the world, but constructs a part of it itself. Such is the position of *Constructive Realism*, which thereby opposes an analytical perception of science. It describes scientific research as a process that creates its own study object. It therefore uses the term "microworlds" in this context.[16] The central claim of Constructive Realism is that we "[can] now understand what we have constructed. We

[12] Kluge 1989, p. 294
[13] «Erkenntnistheorie», in: *Enzyklopädie der Neuzeit* 2005, p. 443
[14] «Erkenntnis», in: *Brockhaus* 1996, p. 534
[15] «Erkenntnis», in: *Brockhaus* 1996, p. 534
[16] "Naturwissenschaftliche Arbeit stellt nicht eine Beschreibung von etwas dar, sondern naturwissenschaftliche Arbeit ist immer konstruktiv. Wenn man z. B. den Menschen, die in Laboratorien arbeiten zusieht, oder ihnen nicht nur zusieht, sondern sie interviewt und mit ihnen ihre Arbeit bespricht, so werden diese Menschen nie von sich aus sagen, dass sie etwas beschreiben. Sie beschreiben nichts. Beschreiben ist Ideologie. (...). Sie machen mit Hilfe theoretischer Erfindungen bzw. logischen Phantasien, wie es Einstein genannt hat, die physikalische Theoretiker eingeführt haben, machen sie das, was wir im Konstruktiven Realismus 'Mikrowelten' nennen. Die Wissenschaftler konstruieren die Daten, die sie aus der Arbeit der Experimentatoren haben, verbinden diese Daten, setzen diese Daten in ein 'framework', in eine Struktur, in eine logische Struktur, die frei erfunden wurde. Das ist eine schöne Arbeitsteilung. Das hat nichts mit Objektivität zu tun, das hat nichts mit Beschreibung zu tun, ist aber natürlich faszinierend." Wallner 1997, p. 21

[17] Wallner 1997, p. 23

[18] Camartin, Iso, «Die Geisteswissenschaften, Relikt der Vergangenheit
oder Rezept für die Zukunft?», in:
Schweizerische Hochschulkonferenz
1991, p. 44–45

[19] Bonsiepe, 2004, p. 16

[20] «Science is analytic; design is constructive.» Cross, Nigel, «Design Method and
scientific method», in: Jacques 1980, p. 18

[21] Feyerabend 1984, p. 190–191

[22] "Seit den späten 1950er Jahren hat
sich die Wissenschaftstheorie aber dem
Thema der Theoriendynamik, des *Wandels*
des wissenschaftlichen Wissens geöffnet,
sie zieht das *experimentelle*, nicht in
Theorien kodierte wissenschaftliche
Wissen und überhaupt Wissenschaft als
Praxis stärker in Betracht und sie knüpft
stärker als in ihrer frühen Phase an tra-
ditionelle philosophische Fragestellungen
und Diskussionen der Erkenntnistheorie,
Sprachphilosophie, Naturphilosophie
und Metaphysik an." Bartels 2007, p. 7

[23] "Es geht nicht mehr so sehr darum,
was Wissenschaftler sagen und was sie
als ihre wissenschaftlichen Resultate
präsentieren, sondern wie sie dorthin
gelangen, was sie machen; und es geht
auch nicht mehr so sehr um die Rekonstruktion eines logischen, rationalen
Denkwegs oder eine Theorie, sondern um
das Abschreiten des unübersichtlichen,
von Nebenwegen und Unvorherse-
hbarkeiten gesäumten Geländes der
wissenschaftlichen Praxis." Hagner,
Michael, in: Rheinberger 1997, p. 341

[24] "Malgré la richesse, la confusion, l'am-
biguïté et la fascination qui se révèlent
ainsi, il est étonnant de constater com-
bien peu nombreux sont ceux qui, venus
de l'extérieur, ont pénétré les rouages
internes de la science et de la technique
et en son ressortis pour en proposer
une explication qui soit compréhensible
au profane et qui ne dépende pas trop
des scientifiques eux-mêmes." Latour
1995, p. 50

cannot understand anything else."[17] So knowledge can only be achieved through one's own "deeds", or actions and manipulations. This perception of scientific research as the construction of some-thing real, as well as an understanding of knowledge as the result of a process, is very important for architects, since it adresses the question of the relevant fields' relationship with reality. Different forms of research also describe "different forms of human curios-ity."[18] In principal, the idea remains that the human sciences describe the world and that natural science attempts to prove it. Human and natural sciences would approach reality from the perspective of what can be recognised, while the architect approaches it from the perspective of what can be conceived. So human and natural sciences bring new cognition, while an architect's design process creates new experiences.[19] This theory by Gui Bonsiepe is also supported by Nigel Cross when he states that science is analytical and design is constructive.[20] But Constructive Realism refuses to make precisely such distinctions when it states that science "designs".
Another example of undermining the rationalist perception of science can be found in the way the rationalist ambition of science was relativised. Albert Einstein and Max Planck both argued that the-ories and terms are fictions of the impossibility of a scientific copy of reality.[21] Questioning the ability of science to copy or construct leads us to question the role of action. Thus experimentation to gain cognition increasingly becomes the focus of attention in scientific theory.
This in turn leads to greater interest in the processes that achieved a specific result and consequently to action itself.[22] Michael Hagner for instance stresses how the emphasis increasingly shifts from the result to the question of which path the research takes.[23] The French sociologist Bruno Latour deserves mention in this context, since he worked on such processes (and action in science) with the aim of making them clear even to those without knowledge.[24]
In this way, experiment no longer has the role of confirming a theory. Instead it performs a theory. It thereby loses some of its detached perspective as a passive entity and becomes part of the action.

We especially have Ian Hacking to thank for this concept, as his book *Representing and Intervening*, which was published in 1983, was one of the first to postulate the importance of experiment not only in terms of testing, but also as a performance of theory: "Science is said to have two aims: theory and experiments. Theories try to say how the world is. Experiments and subsequent technology change the world. We represent and we intervene. We represent in order to intervene, and we intervene in the light of representations."[25] In this way, Hacking opened discussion on the role of action not merely as technology, but also a means of creating cognition and simultaneously influencing or constructing reality. This approach takes us back to the empiricism of the 17th and 18th Centuries.

In parallel with this (re-) discovery of action, models of action can be found in science that are anything but rational. The method of "tinkering" is a case in point, describing something that is common to the scientist and a designer.[26] Anther example is the idea of two different forms of cognition, one scientific and one mythical, as proposed in the mythical and technical thought of Claude Lévi-Strauss. He explains this distinction by comparing *bricoleurs* with *ingenieurs*.[27]

This highlights the fact that however much action in scientific research is permitted to be aleatory and based on tinkering, it must all the more then conform with the criteria of science and be explained by theory. At that point if not before, the creative process of architecture diverges from the path of scientific research. To a certain extent, design is not communicable, nor is it traceable, whereas research must be both.

Due to the emphasis on construction and action in science, some authors have gone as far as describing science as a form of design. They thereby underline its proximity to architectural design. Ranulph Glanville for instance states that (scientific) research is a design activity.[28]

The following can be concluded on the relationship between knowledge and action: Either knowledge controls the action or action produces knowledge. Their relationship "can no longer be (presented) using principles of linear causality, instead at best using those

[25] Hacking 1983, p. 31

[26] Dieser Begriff stammt vom Philosophen Kantorovich, nach Bonsiepe, 2004, p. 17

[27] Lévi-Strauss 1997, p. 29–30

[28] "(Scientific) research (whether experiment or theory) is a design activity. We design experiments, but we also act as designers in how we act in these experiments. We design the experiences and objects we find through experiment by finding commonalities (simplification): and we design how we assemble them into patterns (explanatory principles, theories). Looking at these patterns, we make further patterns from them – the theories of our theories. Thus, in doing science, we learn." Glanville 1999, p. 10

[29] Mandl 2000, p. 222

[30] "The segregation now prevalent for several decades between action research and mainstream social research has not always been the case. In fact, action research originated from 'hard core' social science, i.e. from the experimentalism of Kurt Lewin and John Dewey". In: Berg 2008, S. 7–8

[31] "Action research was originally conceived as an extension and development of mainstream experimental research. But by making experimentation less formalistic, less manipulative, and more participative, action research was soon alienated from the currents of social research constituting the mainstream at the time. It challenged the fundamental division between the researchers and the researched and the control over so called 'independent variables' supposed to secure among other things the kind o objectivity one tries to obtain in 'real' sciences." Berg, Anne Marie, Eikeland Olav, "Organizational Theory and Action Research – Antagonism, Indifference, or Attraction?", in: Berg 2008, p. 7–8

[32] Stringer, 2007, p. 8

[33] Lewin 1968, p. 112

[34] "Action Research is a collaborative approach to inquiry or investigation that provides people with the means to take systematic action to resolve specific problems." Stringer 2007, p. 8

[35] Strübing 2008, p. 13

[36] Strübing 2008, p. 14

[37] "Kunst", in: Mittelstrass 1980–1996, p. 513

[38] "Wesentlich scheint zunächst eine grundlegende Frage: die der Vereinbarkeit von künstlerischem Handeln und wissenschaftlichem Denken unter der Fragestellung der Erkenntnis." Kämpf-Jansen 2001, p. 3

of systemic causality". Furthermore: "Knowledge and action are organised in multilayered ways. Those responsible for their processes are in important cases (though not always) both individual and mutually interwoven social systems (...)."[29] The complexity and significance of this relationship is especially clear in architecture.

Hybrid forms of research

Even within scientific research, models exist that do not conform with the canon and are described in this study as hybrids. *Action Research* is one example. The origins of Action Research lie in the work by Kurt Lewin in 1944.[30] It was his aim to develop research that was less formal and more related to the object.[31] It is basically structured in a 3-phase model – "Look, Think, Act"[32] – and has a circular or spiral shape. Lewin defines his intentions in an essay written in 1939 as follows: "I am convinced it is possible to experiment in sociology in a way that has the same right to be called scientific experiment as in physics or chemistry."[33] It should be stressed however that *Action Research* is not research *through* experiment – as it is often mistakenly described. Instead, it is a type of research that can produce a design in the sense of a (mostly social) action that is the answer to a specific problem.[34] An equally hybrid form of research also stems from social studies and is known as *Grounded Theory*, a research form or rather "style of research to handle theories based on empirical theories".[35] It also allows action to play an important role, since *Grounded Theory* is defined as a "practically, interactively achieved activity".[36]

"Aesthetic research" is also worth mentioning, since it postulates a form of intuitive, non-discursive or sensual research from which knowledge is gained. Aesthetic or sensual research expresses itself in "artistic action".[37] It is based on the theory of aesthetics by the German philosopher Alexander Gottlieb Baumgartner and builds its understanding of research on a direct relationship between the subject and object. At the same time, aesthetic research cannot do without rational research, which strongly undermines its independence.[38]

The following quote by Helga Kämpf-Jansen is paradigmatic for the "incomplete" nature of this form of research: "The hope to find in the field of aesthetics a form of cognition that is not the result of conceptual thought is great. The promise of sensual cognition plays a part: Only using the senses – seeing and painting, hearing and making music, feeling and forming, combined with olfactory delight and sensory-motor experiences, it should be possible to achieve a form of cognition that lies beyond cold reason."[39]

In *The new production of knowledge, The dynamics of science and research in contemporary societies* by Michael Gibbons and a group of other authors, which was published in 1994, a distinction is made between conventional and hybrid forms of research. The authors use "Mode 1" and "Mode 2" in the book to describe two ways of gaining cognition, whereby their interest lies mainly in developing *Mode 2*. While *Mode 1* is principally disciplinary and conventional, *Mode 2* is transdisciplinary and dependent on the application context.[40] For Gibbons, *Mode 2* is already a description of architectural research. However it should be pointed out that the book hardly goes beyond a statement of intent, which has often been criticised.

Knowledge/Experience

An emphasis on action in gaining cognition leads to new perceptions with respect to experience. Every repeated action generates experience. If this action proves to be research, the resulting cognition can hardly be distinguished between experience and knowledge. This is particularly the case in architecture.

The question of a more precise definition of knowledge in connection with experience has been widely discussed. Even in ancient times, Aristotle distinguished between action and production: Action is an end in itself while production is always linked to an end.[41] He explains this dichotomy using the example of building, whereby he also refers to the question of ability.[42]

In the 20th Century, the English philosopher Bertrand Russell wrote a chapter of his book entitled *The problems of Philosophy* (published 1912) that was dedicated to distinguishing between what he described as "knowledge by acquaintance" and "knowledge by description". Knowledge by acquaintance is a direct knowledge that we gain

[39] Kämpf-Jansen 2001, p. 12

[40] "In Mode 1 problems are set and solved in a context governed by the, largely academic, interest for a specific community. By contrast, Mode 2 knowledge is carried out in a context of application. Mode 1 is disciplinary while Mode 2 is transdisciplinary. Mode 1 is characterised by homogeneity, Mode 2 by heterogeneity. Organisationally, Mode 1 is hierarchical and tends to preserve its for, while Mode 2 is more heterarchical and transient. Each employs a different type of quality control. In comparison with Mode 1, Mode 2 is more socially accountable and reflexive. It includes a wider, more temporary and heterogeneous set of practitioners, collaborating on a problem defined in a specific and localized context." Gibbons 1994, p. 3

[41] Aristoteles 2003, p. 155–156

[42] Aristoteles 2003, p. 158

[43] "We shall say that we acquaintance with anything of which we are directly aware, without the intermediary of any process of inference or any knowledge of truths." Russell 1998, p. 25

[44] "This describes the table by means of the sense-data. In order to know anything at all about the table, we must know truths connecting it with things with which we have acquaintance: we must know that 'such-and-such sense data are caused by a physical object'. (...). We know a description, and we know that there is just one object to which this description applies, though the object itself is not directly known to us. In such a case, we say that our knowledge of the object is knowledge by description." Russell 1998, p. 26

[45] "Knowing that is the knowledge which can be made explicit, which can be formulated into advice, into procedures or into organized rules of conventional wisdom. Or example, an architect knows that so many square meters of space are necessary (by convention) to a four-person house. Similarly he knows that a minimum sized bathroom will occupy a floor area of 2 m x 2 m using standard sanitary ware. He knows that drains should fail at a minimum gradient of 1:40, and so on. Knowing how cannot be made explicit. It is that tacit knowledge which 'we know but cannot tell'. The architect's 'know-how' derives from the experience of planning and designing and constructing many houses, in discovering subtle tactics within the rules, of finding incidental, spontaneous ways of subverting the rules to greater benefit." Cross 1980, p. 25–26

[46] "Zudem beschrieb 1958 der Biochemiker und Philosoph Michael Polanyi erstmals ein stilles Wissen als *Tacit knowledge*. Es handelt sich um ein Wissen, das weder formalisierbar noch in wissenschaftliche Forschung zu übersetzen ist. Es geht dabei um die Akkumulation von Wissen."
Heymann 2005, S. 30

without any form of communication.[43] Knowledge by description is knowledge gained by the description of an object.[44]

A later example can be found in the work of Gilbert Ryle, who distinguishes between "knowing how" and "knowing that", especially in his book *The concept of the mind* published in 1949. *Knowing how* is knowledge one can explain, while *knowing that* is not.[45] In the German translation, the terms *Können* and *Wissen* were used, with a note on the insufficient nature of these terms. The distinction is increasingly stressed in general discussion on research in architecture.[46]

Work by the sociologist Anthony Giddens also contains a study of the question of experience with a distinction between discursive and practical consciousness. Unlike the practical, the discursive denotes a consciousness one can describe in words.[47]

All these models are evidence of the need to distinguish between knowledge based on research and knowledge based on experience. This stresses the great significance of the forms of knowledge achieved through action. To conclude this look at different forms of knowledge generation and research, we refer to the work on craftsmanship by Richard Sennet. His theory in discourse is "to do is to think".[48] The theory of *Prehension* is especially important for this study. In it, Sennet desribes the parallels between the spiritual and physical grasping of things.[49]

Research through design

The step from the above mentioned models of experience to research in architecture can be found in Glanville, who suggests a distinction between *knowledge for* and *knowledge of* in the field of architecture. He thereby attempts to define the specific form of knowledge for architecture – a knowledge *for* architecture, rather than a knowledge *of* architecture. Although this distinction is very fitting, it does not seem plausible since according to our understanding, knowledge for design is based on knowledge of architecture.

Architecture as research generates cognition and knowledge that cannot *per se* be compared to other forms of knowledge. Architectural knowledge is achieved through action and the manipulation of space, and can only be communicated to a limited extent using language. Thus the designer is limited in using words to describe the process, which is a precondition for scientific traceability.

This consideration is confirmation for us in our attempt to establish a specific architectural knowledge. In discussing what is here described as spatial knowledge, a parallel can be drawn with the so-called knowledge of images. In this context, the terms *iconic* or *pictorial turn* are used, whereby the "primacy of discursivity as a privileged space is broken by knowledge".[50] The *turn* is aimed at recognising a specific cognition that generates production and the use of images. "Images allow cognition to take shape. It becomes concrete, is moulded and becomes tangible."[51] The result is a distinct form of knowledge or a "visual competence or ability to use and interpret images, as well as to talk about images."[52]

Like images, we believe that space must also be regarded as an independent form of knowledge, both in terms of its production and its communication. Philippe Boudon speaks of the absence of a "conceptual space" in architecture, in the sense of a lacking ability to grasp and describe architectural space.[53]

[47] Giddens 1997, p. 36
[48] Sennett 2008, p. 393
[49] Sennett 2008, p. 207
[50] Bonsiepe 2004, p. 24
[51] Dombois, "Das Design am Übergang von naturwissenschaftlicher und künstlerischer Forschung", in: Forschungslandschaften im Umfeld des Designs 2005, p. 45
[52] Rauhut, Burkhard, "Grusswort", in: Beyer 2005, p. 9
[53] Boudon 1991, p. 15

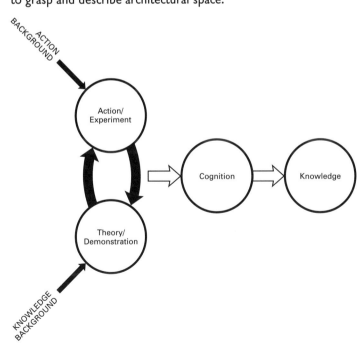

54 "So far I have concentrated on designerly ways of knowing that are embodied in the *processes* of designing. But there is an equally important area of knowledge embodied in the *products* of designing." Cross 2006, p. 9

55 See also the statement by Florian Dombois, who appeals to Swiss funding institutions such as the KTI, SNF and DORE to "also accept non-verbal forms of presentation as research results," and thereby to adapt the application format fort he specific nature of design knowledge. The statement addresses the difficulty of justifying and describing such a form of knowledge. Dombois, Florian, "Das Design am Übergang von Naturwissenschaftlicher und künstlerischer Forschung", in: Forschungslandschaften im Umfeld des Designs 2005, p. 50–51

Space and its production, including the instruments used for their creation form such knowledge resulting from architecture as research. Cross stresses how the architect's knowledge can not only be found in the process, but also in the products.[54] Knowledge in the process however seems to belong to a different order from knowledge of the product. Knowledge in the process assumes in the observer the presence of what one could call a "spatial code". By contrast, the knowledge in a product reveals little of the production process and its instruments, and has countless different interpretation methods, such as symbolism. However they hardly contain signs of knowledge.[55]

As part of this study, a diagram was developed with the aim of achieving a deeper understanding of knowledge and the process of research in architecture. In a first step, it was attempted to present the conventional process of scientific research. In this conventional understanding of research and science, theory and action/experiment interacts to create knowledge. The process, which can move in a circular direction with many steps forward and backwards, leads to cognition, which in turn generates knowledge.

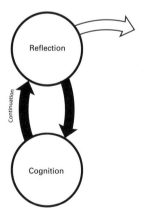

Research on architecture

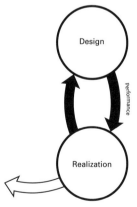

Architectural work

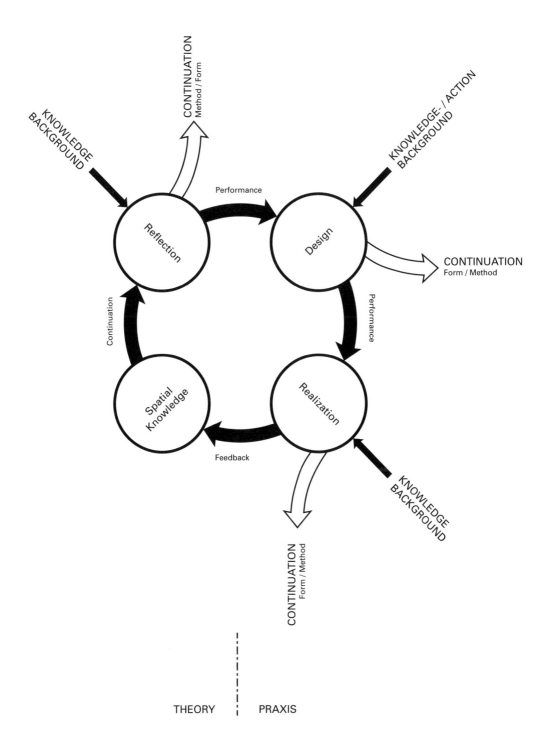

CONTINUATION
Method / Form

KNOWLEDGE
BACKGROUND

KNOWLEDGE- / ACTION
BACKGROUND

Performance

Reflection

Design

CONTINUATION
Form / Method

Continuation

Performance

Spatial
Knowledge

Realization

Feedback

KNOWLEDGE
BACKGROUND

CONTINUATION
Form / Method

THEORY ┊ PRAXIS

[56] "Finally, as several design researchers have pointed out, sketches in design promote the recognition of emergent features and properties of the solution concept. They help the designer to make what Goel (1995) called 'lateral transformations' in the solution space: the creative shift to new alternatives. They assist in what Goldschmidt (1991) called the 'dialectics of sketching', the dialogue between 'seeing that' and 'seeing as', where 'seeing that' is reflective criticism and 'seeing as' is the analogical reasoning and reinterpretation of the sketch that, again, provokes creativity." Cross 2006, p. 37

Based on the diagram, a circular system is proposed for architecture, which spans across design, implementation, spatial knowledge and reflection. Depending on the architect, the starting point may differ, while a different approach can move in a new direction.

The elements of reflection upon, design and implementation of the background to the knowledge and action also have an influence. This background includes personal experience – what influences the architect himself – and also experiences resulting from the repetition of the creative architectural process. The former determines the personal understanding of architecture, while the latter allow the architect to draw from a specific active experience for every new task.

Spatial knowledge is an individual aspect and simultaneously the result of this process. Unlike declaratory, procedural and conditional knowledge, such spatial "inventive knowledge" is able to constantly find solutions for new situations. Such "inventive knowledge" is also based on experience.

Research regards itself as the search for instruments and methods to solve a specific problem and implement a specific intention at hand. This intention can no longer be compared to a scientific theory that is tested. Instead it consists of personal parameters and defined parameters such as the programmes and legal and technical limitations.

In the following chapter, the introduced model is applied to several case studies in a field study. It shows what connection between intention and design instrument exists and to what extent new instruments and methods have been sought or already exist and have been adapted. Instruments and methods are regarded as standard instruments of architecture such as models, plans and sketches, as well as new ones such as diagrams and algorithms. Each of these instruments has a specific role and function for architectural research with respect to structuring the way to a solution in transforming ideas into forms and space.[56]

A distinction must be made between instruments that serve to create form and those that serve communication using a form. In this context, Gerd de Bruyn fittingly explains the difference between sketching and notation. It lies in the fact that a sketch needs only to be legible for the artist that produced it (in a kind of private language), while notation must be legible for third parties (in a kind of universal language).[57] A similar differentiation and specification must be applied to all instruments. Since an ever-increasing number of architects produce their designs in interdisciplinary groups, the question of the role of an exchange of knowledge arises. Relatively few theoretical approaches to this aspect currently exist.

To conclude, the significance of research through architecture and its instruments must also be studied with respect to the communication of such knowledge in teaching. How can an architect communicate his knowledge to a student if he is not fully aware of it himself? Two models can be distinguished in this respect: Either the students practice replicating the exact method and task (intention) of the architect, or they are forced to develop their own working methods through the highest degree of freedom. In the first case, the hope is to produce a learning effect from a mimetic stance and thereby achieve a greater understanding of the master. The second method forces a selective observation of role models to directly develop one's own style. In this context, Cross[58] appeals to the responsibility of the teacher to communicate his knowledge.

[57] De Bruyn 2008, p. 24–25

[58] "What designers know about their own problem-solving processes remains largely tacit knowledge – *i.e.* they know it in the same way that a skilled person 'knows' how to perform that skill. They find it difficult to externalise their knowledge, and hence design education is forced to rely so heavily on an apprenticeship system of learning. It may be satisfactory, or at least understandable, for practicing designers to be inarticulate about their skills, but teachers of design have a responsibility to be as articulate as they possibly can about what it is they trying to teach, or else they can have no basis for choosing the content and methods of their teaching." Cross 2006, p. 9

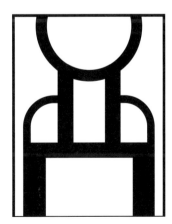

Field Studies

The following architects were chosen as examples for the field studies below: Jean Prouvé, Aldo Rossi, Peter Eisenman, Christopher Alexander and Peter Zumthor. The selection of these study preparations was based on the distinctive approaches of the relevant protagonists, with working processes that are weighted on a number of points in varying orders on the diagram. This allows us to present as wide a spectrum of approaches as possible. The relevant working processes have the common aspect of a conscious search for ways to implement their highly individual intentions in architecture.

The diagram can be used to comprehensively illustrate the individual process. It presents the flow of knowledge and highlights what knowledge is created at which points. It records how spatial knowledge is generated and forwarded to the next step in the process. The danger of simplification is met by the fact that it is a model rather than a blueprint of the creative architectural process. The model illustrates without necessarily reducing or questioning the dynamism of the process, in fact the contrary. It can be assumed that the cycle of the diagram is repeated several times and that individual moments during the architect's creative process presented here could have taken a different course. The model is particularly valuable in presenting possible flows of knowledge in the process. It provides the ideal basis to experiment and invites one to assess one's own or the studied action. In this way, any arising spatial knowledge can be tested for its communicability and sustainability.

The concluding notes at the end of the field study synthesise the results. A glossary of the most important definitions and terms in this study supports the field study.

Glossary

Intention

A not necessarily verbally formulated aim to spatially implement one's own ideas in architecture. This aim need not be project or context-related. The mere questioning of architecture can be regarded as an intention. The intention is analogous to a research interest and it can be assumed that no research occurs without intention.

Implementation

Carrying out a design as a constructed project. Executing an idea or concept in the field of construction.

Performance

Implementation/performance of a concept – knowledge, theory or design – both in a theoretical and a practical framework. Performance can, but need not be implementation.

Design

The Middle High German *entwerfen* initially means 'artistically execute' (painting, inlaying, embroidery, stitching etc.); later influenced by the Latin *proiectare* and French *projeter*, to throw down a quick, fleeting sketch."[1] In architecture, the design includes the creation of a project with specific circumstances and intentions that can then be implemented.

[1] Kluge 1989, p. 181
[2] Kluge 1989, p. 185
[3] "Erfahrung", in: Mittelstrass 1980–1996, p. 569

Experience

German *erfahren*, "originally 'travelling through', then 'getting to know a country'".[2] In colloquial language, "experience means the acquired ability of orientation, being familiar with specific relationships of actions and facts without recourse to any theoretical knowledge that is independent of it."[3] Experience is the opposite of research and like it creates knowledge, whereby knowledge that

[4] Kluge 1989, p. 294
[5] Kluge 1989, p. 311
[6] Beyer 2005, p. 470
[7] "Experiment", in: Jäger 2005, p. 724
[8] Beyer 2005, p. 470
[9] Beyer 2005, p. 471

stems from experience cannot be formulated. Experience is personal and cannot be communicated. Both practice and theory can be based on a background experience, from which the designer can draw.

Cognition

The German *Erkenntnis*, "what is recognised, insight, identifying, grasping reality."[4] A distinction is made between evident and intuitive cognition, whereby the former is methodical, conceptual and communicated. The latter is uncommunicated and sensually structured. There are two fundamental types of cognition: rational and empirical. Rational cognition has gained the upper hand as a result of the scientific dominance of our society. Empiricism sees the origin of cognition in the senses, while rationalism sees it in thought. Very recent scientific theories require the previous existence of a background action for both types of cognition to occur. The opposite of cognition is cognisance, which, like experience, is not communicable.

Experiment/Action

"Attempt, trial, proof, (noun derived from Latin verb *experiri*, to try, to attempt)."[5]

The experiment opposes observation and is an instrument of empiricism, i.e. sensual research. Unlike observation, "the result is deliberately and plannably achieved under controlled, reduced and replicable conditions."[6] Using an experiment, the objects are manipulated with the aim of gaining new cognition on them or confirming existing knowledge. A distinction is made between *experimentum* – individual experiences – and *experienta* – general experience.[7] The experiment basically serves to test a hypothesis, whereby the expectations of the experimenter must not influence the results."[8] In natural sciences, the experiment is "causally oriented", whereby the focus lies in the "relationship between cause and effect."[9] The experiment is used to test a theory, but also to perform a theory, and this performance may succeed or fail. In addition to theories, it can generally be aimed at performing an idea. In that case, the experiment cannot initially be completely planned, but must be

a posteriori. Ian Hacking places experiment and theory in opposition to each other and stresses that, just as theory aims to explain the world, experiment aims to change it, whereby both actions are closely interwoven.[10] Hacking rediscovered the constructive nature of experimentation.[11]

While experimentation is also regarded as the performance of a theory, the performances in the architecture cycle defined here can be described as experiments.

Research

"Seeking cognition, exploring."[12] Research describes a planned and target-oriented process, the results of which must be general and provable. A distinction is made between underlying research, applied research and experimental research.

A methodical distinction is made between deduction (top-down method) and induction (bottom-up method). Another method, abduction, was developed by Charles Sanders. In addition to traditional scientific and discursive research, "sensual" research is also reperformed, using experiment and observation. Sensual research is an instrument of art, among other fields. Both forms of research lead to cognition, the difference being that scientific research leads to the cognition of cognition (metacompetence of the second level).[13]

Research moves between trusted and innovative methods, whereby the latter is a reaction to a specific innovative pressure.

The precondition of architectural research as defined here is the communicability of the spatial experience resulting from the cyclically structured process.

Sustainability

In science, knowledge must be "traceable, testable and usable,"[14] thereby expressing its sustainability. In architecture, sustainability is not based on traceability, but on its ability to be received, which is in turn a precondition for architecture as research and the related spatial knowledge.

In architecture, sustainability therefore means the ability to continue methods or take over the forms of an architect. Accordingly,

[10] "Science is said to have two aims: theory and experiments. Theories try to say how the world is. Experiments and subsequent technology change the world. We represent and we intervene. We represent in order to intervene, and we intervene in the light of representations." Hacking 1983, p. 30

[11] "Im 19. Jh. fand experimentelle Forschung erstmals institutionelle Formen, angetrieben durch die zunehmend erkennbare praktische Bedeutung der Naturwissenschaften. Um die Jahrhundertmitte waren experimentelle Verfahren in der Chemie fest institutionalisiert; in den physikalischen Wissenschaften, der Physiologie (Experimentalmedizin) und der Psychologie fanden ähnliche Entwicklungen zeitverzögert in der zweiten Jahrhunderthälfte statt. Für das neu aufkommende Selbstbewusstsein der modernen naturwiss. Disziplinen spielte das E. eine zentrale Rolle. (...). Obgleich in der Forschungspraxis immer eine Vielfalt unterschiedlicher experimenteller Arbeitsweisen praktiziert wurde, von denen die Theorieprüfung nur eine darstellte, sollte diese Standardauffassung zum E. erst in den 1980er Jahren unter Kritik geraten. In der noch andauernden Diskussion geht es um Fragen zum konstruktiven Charakter des E., zur Rolle experimenteller Artefakte und zu kulturellen und sozialen Funktionen des E., aber ganz zentral – und das ist bezeichnend – auch um die schon im 17. Jh. aufgeworfenen Fragen nach der Bedeutung der immer nur eingeschränkt möglichen Replizierbarkeit und nach der (induktivern, theorietestenden usw.) Art und Weise des Erkenntnisgewinns aus E." "Experiment", in: Jaeger 2005, p. 726–727

[12] Kluge 1989, p. 581

[13] "Forschung", in: Mittelstrass 1980–1996, p. 533

[14] Balzert 2008, p. 6

[15] Kluge 1989, p. 475
[16] "Methode", in: Mittelstrass 1980–1996, p. 876
[17] "Methode", in: Mittelstrass 1980–1996, p. 879
[18] Kluge 1989, p. 560
[19] "Techne", in: Mittelstrass 1980–1996, p. 214
[20] Kluge 1989, p. 1420
[21] "Dagegen wird für eine methodische Rekonstruktion der Naturwissenschaften leitend, dass diese die Konstitution ihrer Gegenstände bereits technischem Handeln verdanken, von der Beherrschung der Pflanzen- und Tierzüchtung für den Gegenstand der Evolutionsbiologie bis zu den Mess-, Experimentier- und Beobachtungsgeräten von Physik und Chemie." "Technik", in: Mittelstrass 1980–1996, p. 215

a distinction is made between methodical and stylistic sustainability, whereby only the former is a requirement for architecture as research.

Method

"Specific, systematic procedure,"[15] from the Greek for "path."[16] Method is generally connected to scientific research. Depending on the context and aim, a distinction is made between analytical, axiomatic, deductive, hermeneutic, historical, inductive, phenomenological, scholastic, synthetic and transcendental methods.[17] Furthermore, scientific theory distinguishes between trusted and innovative methods.

Practice

"17th Century, derived from the Latin *praxis*, 'process', originally Greek *praxis* (also: acting, doing, action), the Greek *prassein* 'to do, to carry out'. Initially used with the meaning of 'activity, process'; then in the 18th Century, it became the antithesis of theory, to mean experience, actual activity."[18] Practice describes the processes in architecture that are characterised by practical work, such as design and implementation. Practice is often regarded as the opposite of theory – although as early as ancient times, Vitruv defined architecture as the union of *fabrica* (craftsmanship) and *ratiocinatio* (intellectual work) – although the two are so interconnected that they are hardly separable and contemporary scientific theory stresses their mutual influence upon each other.

Reflection

Theoretic basis (proactive) and testing (reactive) of one's own work. Precursor to (scientific theory), analogous with architectural theory and can neither completely determine nor explain action.

Feedback

The ability to test content and methods by means of reflection. Reduction is one of the requirements for the communicability of spatial knowledge, even though it can only be communicated to a limited extent.

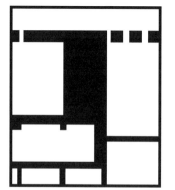

Technology

The term stems from the Greek *Techne*: "ability, art, knowledge, skill."[19] Matthias Heymann defines technology as the "general term for the application of scientific cognition for human society, as well as the methods, processes, instruments and tools it requires."[20] Parallel to the discussion on the significance of action for research, the importance of technology and craftsmanship is stressed for this very action.[21]

In architecture, technology stands for the instruments of design and implementation. The etymology of the term architecture – first craftsman (archi-tékton) – refers to its technical roots.

Theory

"Systematic summary and generalisation of cognition in a (scientific) field, also 'conceptual, abstract point of view.'"[22]

The term stems from *theoros*, the observer sent to the Oracle to report on it.[23] Over time, the term developed as a "purely intellectual consideration of connections... that cannot be sensually perceived.[24] A theory is traditionally regarded as something immovable. A distinction is made between unscientific use, philosophical uses and individual scientific uses, including architectural theory.[25] Architectural theory is basically regarded as "thoughts on architecture"[26] and is a mixture of a *non-scientific use*, as guidance for practice, as a predictor, and of an *individual scientific use*, where it can be regarded as reflection upon practice. In most cases, there is a grey area between them. Architectural theory "seeks to integrate categories of construction in craftsmanship, technology, politics, society and aesthetics in a methodically derived system of statements that mutually justify and support each other," whereby the tense relationship between theory and practice reperforms "a constant challenge for architecture."[27] In the framework of architecture, a basic distinction is made between proactive and reactive theory. The latter reflects upon a design, while the former informs it.[28] In this context, it should be stressed that the theories are architectural rather than scientific. Architectural theory is characterised by the fact that it is not a direct set of instructions for design and that it is closely interwoven with practice.

[22] Kluge 1989, p. 1429

[23] "Der griechische Ursprung des Wortes Theorie, theoria, geht auf die Wurzel theorein: Anschauen, Betrachten zurück. Thea war die Erscheinung, die verstanden werden muss, und theoros der Betrachter, der von einer polis zum Orakel gesendet wurde, um dort anwesend zu sein und darüber mit Autorität, d. h. ohne Änderungen zu berichten. Die Bedeutung der Theorie ist also mit der Berichterstattung des unbeteiligten und objektiven Betrachters verbunden." Moravansky 2008, p. 6

[24] "Theorie", in: Mittelstrass 1980–1996, p. 260

[25] "Theorie", in: Mittelstrass 1980–1996, p. 260–263

[26] "Architekturtheorie", in: Jaeger 2005, p. 587

[27] "Architekturtheorie", in: Jaeger 2005, p. 587

[28] "It seems that one might differentiate between a pro-active theory that aims at informing and stimulating the design process, and re-active theory that rather reflects on the design process and its products. Both forms of theory are present in the European schools of architecture, the first one probably in close connection with the design studio, the second one rather as more autonomous courses. The workshop will focus the pro-active theory, investigating its relationships with the re-active one, questioning their overlaps and differences, and mapping them with respect to the production of architecture as well as to the field of architecture and the related disciplines." *Second EAAE-ENHSA Sub-network Workshop on Architectural Theory*, 2008, p. 1

[29] Kluge 1989, p. 1575
[30] Pfäffli 2005, p. 70
[31] Kluge 1989, p. 1575
[32] "Forschung", in: Jaeger 2005, p. 1061
[33] Mittelstrass 1980–1996, p. 719–721
[34] "Theorien und Lehren, die sich der Kritik und Überprüfung entziehen, und damit den wissenschaftlichen Qualitätsanforderungen nicht genügen, sind nicht-wissenschaftlich. Wird ihnen dennoch ein wissenschaftlicher Anstrich gegeben, spricht man von 'Pseudowissenschaften'." Balzert 2008, S. 18

Knowledge

"Cognition achieved through research and experience (...)."[29] Like cognition, knowledge is set against opinion and belief. A distinction is made between discursive and intuitive knowledge. Knowledge can not only be gained through research, but can also be created through experience, as in the case of architecture. Knowledge can be classified as declarative, procedural, conditional and inventive, whereby the last form is "to recognise the unique nature of new challenging tasks and if necessary to develop a solution."[30]

The architect's knowledge, which is inventive, is described here as spatial knowledge and comprises the knowledge springing from the creation of space – both real and virtual. Spatial knowledge can only be verbally communicated to a limited extent, especially because it is not only based on research, but also on experience.

Science

"(organised) form of investigating, gathering and assessing cognition."[31] Science is the "planned shaping of research to develop science."[32]

Science is a "term for an orientation in life and the world that requires a special, often professionally executed practice of substantiation and therefore goes beyond everyday knowledge available to everyone. It is the action that produces scientific knowledge."[33] Research activities that do not conform with scientific criteria, but nevertheless insist upon them, are known as "pseudo-sciences".[34] Architecture cannot be a pseudo-science if one describes it as alternative forms of knowledge rather than an alternative science. Architecture is not a science, although it refers to scientific processes – construction physics, supporting structure etc. – but cannot be entirely explained or grasped in rational terms.

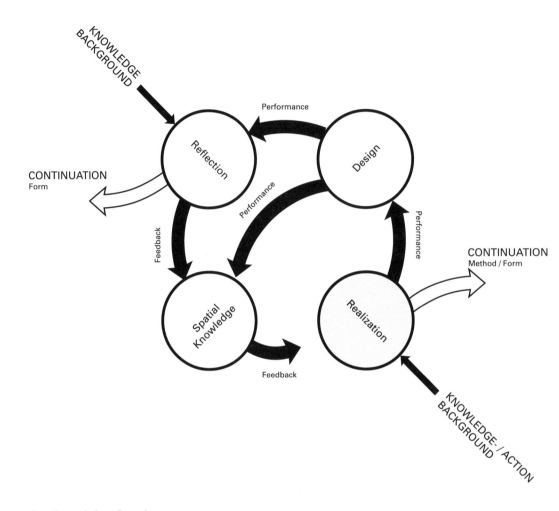

Creative cycle Jean Prouvé

Knowledge-/action background
– Handcraft education to locksmith
– School of Nancy

Realization
– Production

Continuation
– Teaching at CNAM
– Patents
– Participation to CIAM

Design
– Constructive, process-oriented design
– Planning

Reflection
– Systematisation
– Patents

Continuation
– "industrialised style"

Jean Prouvé
(1901–1984)

The guidelines of my work
(...) The guidelines were originally determined by the example of my father and the 'École de Nancy'. This group of creative spirits dedicated itself completely to the task of creating a contemporary environment. I spent my childhood in the midst of it and it led me to live as a man of my time in an uncompromising manner: on the one hand through scientific development that influences all technology, on the other through information, studying the materials and their processing, also through the observation of those who apply them, through the search for inspiration and the right decisions from technology, through the principle of never procrastinating, which reduces momentum, and also by not designing Utopian impossibilities.
(...) I was able to apply these principles until 1950.[1]

Jean Prouvé during his training.
In: Guidot 1990, p. 104

Implementation

Jean Prouvé's architectural work is aimed at producing (construction) elements. In his opinion, the process of production played a decisive role in design. Only what can be produced, implemented and assembled is worth being developed.[2] In his work, Prouvé starts with implementation and subordinates the other creative processes beneath it. This rather unusual approach can clearly be explained by his family situation and his personal career.

Jean Prouvé was born in Paris on April 8, 1901. His father, a painter and sculptor who was active in a wide range of fields, was a close friend of Émile Gallé, who founded the École de Nancy. Convened the year Jean Prouvé was born, the École de Nancy's aim was an *Alliance provinciale des industries d'art*, uniting various producers, craftsmen of all kinds, architects, intellectuals and art critics under the chairmanship of Gallé. Together, not only art, but also a large number of everyday objects were to be produced for the general public in close collaboration with traditional craftsmanship and industrial production. Jean Prouvé, the godson of the extremely

[1] Prouvé, Huber, Steinegger 1971, p. 10
[2] Prouvé, Huber, Steinegger 1971, p. 11

[3] For instance a fence for the in 1927 Haus Reifenberg, architect R. Mallet-Stevens.

Prouvé-Sheds for the Mame printing house in Tours, 1950
In: Vegesack (Ed.), 2006, p. 228

active Gallé, grew up in this environment and was later able to uphold many of the ideas and principles in his own work. Between 1916 and 1919, Jean Prouvé completed an apprenticeship as a blacksmith in the forge of Émile Robert in Enghien, followed by another two years' training at the Szabo forge in Paris. Even during his military service immediately afterwards, Prouvé participated in exhibitions with his own smithery at the École des Beaux-Arts in Nancy. After founding his own workshop in 1924, he contributed to numerous other exhibitions, constantly modernised his business and established contact with architects, for whom he produced various pieces of work.[3] In 1931, Prouvé expanded his workshop, which also produced the furniture he developed from 1929 onwards. Between 1935 and 1936, he collaborated with the architects E. Beaudouin and M. Lods to construct the Roland Garros aviation club building in Buc. The most reviewed building by Prouvé is the 'Maison du peuple' in Clichy, which was built between 1935 and 1939 together with the same architects and includes a covered market.

Following active participation in the Résistance and a shift to emergency production during the war years, Jean Prouvé was briefly in politics in 1944 as the Mayor of Nancy.

In 1947, the Atelier Jean Prouvé moved to Maxéville due to the ideal infrastructural conditions there. In 1949, the business changed its structure: l'Aluminium francais acquired a stake in the company and subsequently some products were exclusively produced by it. Despite the overflowing order books in the workshops and many awards for his works, Jean Prouvé finally left the factory in Maxéville in 1953 following serious conflict with his new partners.

Never again was he able to fulfil his ideals of indivisible collaboration between designers and producers in the same way. In the following years, he developed numerous facades and buildings for l'Aluminium francais and other companies – albeit separated from their workshops, in the relevant design departments.

The background to his knowledge, or in his case also activity, is mainly provided by Prouvé's complete training as a craftsman. His extremely advanced, positive attitude towards industrialisation is also centrally important.[4] Jean Prouvé not only had in-depth knowledge of materials – above all metals, as one would expect from a blacksmith – but also of production methods and state of the art tools. The euphoric mood of the growth region around Nancy, with a booming economy, had as much an impact on him as the triumph of the craftwork industry at the Paris World Fair in 1900. A son of the "Nancy Dynasty", as Le Corbusier called it[5], Prouvé was also clearly a representative of his own time. In later appraisals, he was often described as a combined "engineer-architect" with little respect for the boundaries of individual fields. He himself insisted on his role as a 'constructor' and did not intend to blur or dissolve interdisciplinary boundaries.

Design

"Every object to be produced must be preceded by a constructive idea."[6]

The primary aim of Prouvé was to integrate production conditions into the design process. Form should be based on inner character, the structure and correct use, rather than previous aesthetic analysis.[7] The design process therefore is not carried out on the drawing board, but instead requires the observation of practical production. In these observations, it is guided by functionality and above all the properties of the material to be processed. Prouvé spoke of the logic of technical discovery. So prototypes were regarded as a means of planning in the Maxéville workshops, which allowed a way of developing form that took production into account.

Jean Prouvé himself described the right order of tasks in construction as follows:

"a) The idea, either for a building or furniture

b) Dialogue with the implementing personnel using technical sketches

c) A prototype or model

d) Comments, experiments, tests, improvements – and only finally a drawing, the plan for production.

The 'endless' drawing is more expensive than the prototype."[8]

According to the above maxim, ensembles rather than fragments of buildings should be produced. The approach advocated by Prouvé could only be ideally implemented in the specific situation

[4] Scheidegger 1971, S. 12
In a lecture he mentions the necessity to call upon the responsibility of industry and to eliminate old craftsman's techniques and derive a continuum of techniques from more modern methods. Cohen, Jean-Louis, in: Vegesack (Hg.) 2006, p. 49
[5] Paris, January 7, 1964. Prouvé, Huber, Steinegger 1971, p. 176
[6] In a lecture in Brasilia, 1959. Aus Peters 2006, p. 12
[7] Cohen, Jean-Louis, in: Vegesack (Ed.) 2006, p. 49
[8] Prouvé, Huber, Steinegger 1971, p. 13

[9] Prouvé: Signed typoscript, dates September 19, 1953, 9 pages, Fonds Jean Prouvé, ADMM. Herefrom: Coley, Catherine, in: Vegesack, Alexander (Ed.) 2006, p. 123
[10] Coley, Catherine, in: Vegesack (Ed.) 2006, p. 117

he developed for himself in Maxéville. Industrial production in one's own factory was extremely important for his work. At the same time, precisely this attitude led to the irresolvable dispute in the workshops that spelled the end of his work there. The 'empirical creative technique' of Prouvé and its permanently presented ideas and constant feedback between the object and process are much more similar to the conditions and processes of research than those of actual production.

These conditions, which were so unique in Prouvé's workshops, had an economic effect. While the business steadily increased its turnover in the early 1950s, its profits shrunk and the financial situation became critical. An additional extension of the facility due to full-capacity production and the separation of research and development from production and serial manufacturing were desired and initially seemed to be the solution. But the measures actually led to the disappearance of the 'esprit Prouvé' and a technical decline.[9] The new capital investors recognised neither the spirit of the factory nor Prouvé's specific working methods. They perceived a 'stil Prouvé' that was commercially usable for the serial production of elements with diverse uses in the building industry. The new stakeholders therefore failed to recognise the chances that integrating the design process into the production process can offer.

Insight

Jean Prouvé derived his knowledge of rationalising production from his constructive and process-oriented design. He continuously refined the processes and repeatedly gained new insight from the constant comparison between planning and implementation. For him, the primary 'judges' of the quality of the products were those who carried out the production and assembly[10] – not the later users or even an architect.

His insight consequently often flowed into patents, of which Jean Prouvé registered a countless number, acting as a form of communication of his technical and spatial knowledge.

The École de Nancy plays an important role in his background knowledge. In addition to the alliance consisting of a range of people from different crafts and industries to collectively increase

Armchair for the Cité Universitaire, Nancy 1931–1932, drawing, 1965.
In: Sequin Jousse Galerie, 1998, p. 132

the ability of design and production, the École de Nancy also created a strongly artistic environment. As a result of the many intellectuals it included, not only implementation, but also critical reflection played an important role. Jean Prouvé himself never went to university, but grew up with this less academic and more practically oriented school, which provided an ideal environment for the intensive exchange of ideas.

This condition has much to do with Prouvé's family circumstances: His wife studied at the École des Beaux Arts while his father was a Director there. They both supported his work for many years. Moreover his brothers and later nephews, sons and a daughter all worked in the workshops in various ways, leading to very intensive collaboration. So one can also assume a culture of intense exchange and constant reflection in this respect too.

Advertisement for the STUDAL panelled façade. Developed by Ateliers Jean Prouvé. In: Sequin Jousse Galerie, 1998, p. 237

Theory

According to Jean Prouvé, knowledge and innovation should stem from the factories, so he resisted any form of theories on his work. When he studied the work of other architects and engineers, he was far more interested in the form of design plans than in abstract, theoretical assessment. He dissected and systemised the buildings and objects of his time and thereby derived an understanding that was directly rooted in practice. Nevertheless, one can still speak of theoretical reflection in Jean Prouvé in the sense of an analysis and systemisation that is evident in the following cases:

The first moment in which Prouvé reflected upon his work on a theoretical level came in 1953, when he was working on the CIAM Congress in Aux-en-Provence. Together with J. Belmont and M. Silvy, façades in a fixed CIAM grid were described as a whole and in detail, especially from a draughtsman's perspective, including photos of the production. In addition to this trade show, the authors also took their own stance, which they supported using collages. In few words and with many images, they pointed out the importance of technology and the economy in contemporary life. Plate 9 for instance shows sketches of example buildings that already took a first step on the path towards the 'industrialisation of buildings'. A clear distinction is made between prefabrication and the indus-

Importance du technique et de l'economie sur le mode de vie actuel.

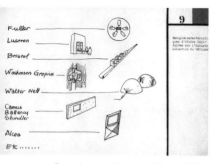

Exemples caractéristiques d' études déjà faites sur l'industrialisation du batiments. Tablets 3 and 9 of the grid developed for the CIAM Congress in Aix-en-Provence, 1953. In: Vegesack (Ed.) 2006, p. 33

[11] Bruno Reichlin, in: Vegesack (Hg.) 2006, p. 29

Jean Prouvé as a teacher at the CNAM, Conservatoire National des Artes et Métiers. CCI Archives Prouvé. In: Guidot 1990, p. 222

trialisation of construction, the former never being an aim of Prouvé's, while the latter is the starting point for his entire work. The CIAM plates clarified the stance and perspective of Jean Prouvé and his team within the entire development process. At the same time, the plates provide a quick dialogue and – albeit with sparse text – a very clear communication of their ideas and products.

In 1958, Jean Prouvé began teaching at the Conservatoire National des Arts et Métiers, C. N. A. M. He took over the Chair for Vocationally Applied Art. In the weekly, well-visited lectures, he constantly drew on the blackboard and illustrated in this way the content and method of how practice precedes theory. Instead of communicating information, he demonstrated his position by explaining constructive principles using examples.[11] This can be described as reflection on action and the communication of knowledge – although always under the primacy of action. Prouvé taught at the CNAM until 1970.

The third moment of theoretical reflection by Jean Prouvé to be mentioned here lies in his collaboration with the publishers Benedikt Huber and Jean-Claude Steinegger for the monograph of his work published in Zurich by Artemis. Both in the book and in the protocols of meetings that were added as individual articles to the catalogue of the Vitra Design Museum, the autobiographer's intensive work with his spatial knowledge is tangible. Above all the catalogue of his construction principles, which was published for the first time in the book and described as an 'alphabet of structures', refers to theoretical work in the form of systemising practical applications. The combining system developed over a period of years and the production processes it entailed are presented in a schematically clarified way.

This too can be described as a very practically oriented stance. The rather unusual approach for architects of his time highlights the fact that Jean Prouvé neither wanted to be an architect nor an engineer. He much rather described himself as an 'homme d'usine', a man of the factory.

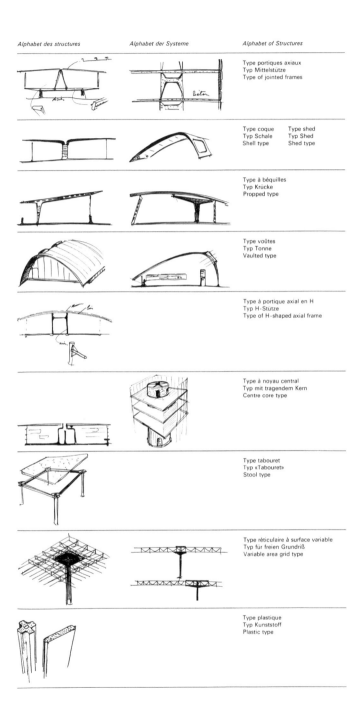

Type portiques axiaux
Typ Mittelstütze
Type of jointed frames

Type coque	Type shed
Typ Schale	Typ Shed
Shell type	Shed type

Type à béquilles
Typ Krücke
Propped type

Type voûtes
Typ Tonne
Vaulted type

Type à portique axial en H
Typ H-Stütze
Type of H-shaped axial frame

Type à noyau central
Typ mit tragendem Kern
Centre core type

Type tabouret
Typ «Tabouret»
Stool type

Type réticulaire à surface variable
Typ für freien Grundriß
Variable area grid type

Type plastique
Typ Kunststoff
Plastic type

Alphabet of systems. In: Prouvé, Huber,
Steinegger (Eds.) 1971, p. 28–29

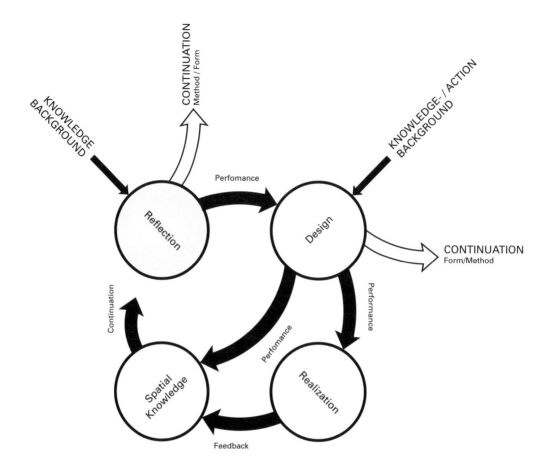

Creative cycle Aldo Rossi

Knowledge background
– Research on the city
– Sociolgy, urban geography, history

Reflection
– Proactive theory
– The architecture of the city/Analysis
  of the city
– Publications

Continuation
– Teaching
– Drawings/images

Knowledge-/action background
– Methods

Design
– Analogy

Realization
– Image

Reflection
– Scientific autobiography

Aldo Rossi
(1931–1997)

Proactive theory

Aldo Rossi is regarded as one of the most influential architects and theoreticians of his generation. Based on his studies of urban typology, he became an important exponent of a new rational approach to architecture and a significant critic of Modernism. He graduated in Architecture at the Milan Polytechnic and began his long collaboration with the architectural journal Casabella-continuità when he was still a student. In 1959 he achieved his PhD at the Milan Polytechnic and opened his own office in the same city. His central book "L'Architettura della città" was published in 1966 and made him a significant critic. Rossi's work is accompanied by continuous teaching, initially in Italy and then increasingly abroad. His teaching at the ETH Zurich is especially relevant to this study. His students included important exponents of the contemporary architectural scene. In 1990, he was awarded the Pritzker Prize for Architecture.

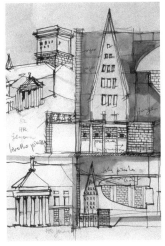

Reconstruction of the Teatro Carlo Felice. Design sketch 1983. In: Rossi 2001, p. 124

Aldo Rossi's publications addressing questions of research, cognition and knowledge forms in architecture as part of his work for Casabella-continuità act as an almost independent background of experience and knowledge for his work. His theoretical considerations achieve their peak in his main work, "L'Architettura della città"[1], which was published in 1966, and the "Autobiografia Scientifica"[2], published in 1981.

Even the introduction to his book, "The architecture of the city", entitled "Urban artefacts and a theory of the city", postulates an understanding of the city as architecture and not as a visible image and sum of its different architectures. Rossi regards the city as an architectural construct covering the entire period of its creation and thereby as a type of collective artefact. Rossi believed that the nature of a city and its construction, its architecture, lies in the contrast between the specific and universal, and between the individual and the collective. In this way, "Rossi advances beyond

[1] Rossi, Aldo, L'Architettura della città, Marsilio 1966, German edition 1973, English edition 1982
[2] Rossi, Aldo, Scientific Autobiography, English edition 1981, Italian edition 1990, German edition 1988

[3] Magnago Lampugnani, Vittorio, "Die Architektur der Stadt als poetische Wissenschaft", in: Becker 2003, p. 51
[4] ebenda
[5] Aldo Rossi was born in Milan in 1931. He studied at the Milan Polytechnic between 1949 and 1959. As early as 1955, he was encouraged to work for the architectural journal Casabella-continuità by Ernesto Nathan Rogers. In 1956 he began to work for Ignazio Gardella and later Marco Zanuso. In 1959, he achieved his doctorate at the Milan Polytechnic. In 1963, Rossi became Assistant to Ludovico Quaroni at the School for Urban Studies in Arezzo and to Carlo Aymonino at the Faculty of Architecture in Venice. In 1965, he became a lecturer at the Milan Polytechnic. His central book "L'Architettura della città" was published in 1966 and made him renowned on an international level. In 1970, he was permanently employed by the Milan Polytechnic. Between 1972 and 1974, he was Guest Professor at the ETH Zurich. During this period (in 1973), he published his theses on "Architettura razionale". In: 1975, he became Professor for Design at Venice University, also teaching and lecturing in the USA, South America, Japan among others. In 1976, his text "La città analoga" and also "Autobiografia scientifica" (Scientific Autobiography), published in 1981. He was awarded the Pritzker Prize for Architecture in 1990. Aldo Rossi died in 1997 following a car accident.
[6] Rossi 1966
[7] Rossi 1988
[8] Werk, Bauen+Wohnen, 12 1997 und 1/2 1998
[9] Ludovico Quaroni, important Italian architect and urbanist, born in Rome in 1911, died 1987.

typological research and moves directly towards architectural design. He creates a connection between analysis and design..."[3] and thereby defines the demand for a scientific approach that "follows objective rather than historical laws".[4]

Moreover Aldo Rossi's "Scientific autobiography" impressively refers to the central significance of his own biography for his architectural work.[5] Aldo Rossi's background experience comprises the above-mentioned theoretical works, his drawings and reflection upon his own implemented buildings. These many influences create a network of interrelationships that makes a homogenous interpretation of his overall work very difficult.

This study focuses on Rossi's theoretical work, especially his two major publications "The architecture of the city"[6] and "Scientific autobiography"[7], as well as Rossi's influence through his teaching work at the ETH Zurich, which is well documented in the journal Werk, Bauen + Wohnen by "Kommentare zur Zürcher Lehrtätigkeit von Aldo Rossi", a retrospective by a number of his "students".[8] This provides the necessary focus for the study and also limits it to Rossi's reception within a Swiss environment, as well as the context of his theoretical work and teaching. The complexity of Aldo Rossi's work, as a theorist, architect and teacher, can only be presented using individual aspects that demonstrate the interaction of knowledge/experience and design and – with reference to the subject of this study – shed light on the scientific bases of Rossi's architectural design work. It is therefore a strictly limited perspective, yet one that directly refers to Aldo Rossi's own theoretical comments, as well as statements by his direct students in the Swiss context.

Rossi's theoretical references are anchored in Italian Rationalism (Razionalismo) and therefore the parallelism of classical Roman and modern design principles, although he has repeatedly stressed his critical distance from it. Ludovico Quaroni[9], Carlo Aymonino[10] and especially Rossi's teacher Ernesto Nathan Rogers[11] made important impacts on his thought. Ernesto Nathan Rogers played a significant role in encouraging Rossi's theoretical and literary discussion on architecture, motivating him to work for the architectural journal

Casabella-continuità, which was a decisive stimulus for his later work.

The first phase

Rossi refers to a large number of sources for his main theoretical work "The architecture of the city"[12], including sociology, urban geography and architectural theory. The central statements of Rossi's theoretical thought can be derived from the titles and sub-titles of the individual chapters, for example in Chapter 1: "The structure of urban artefacts", "The individuality of urban artefacts", "The urban artefact as a work of art", "Typological questions", "Critique of naive functionalism" and "Monuments and the theory of permanence". Rossi's epistemological basis is especially expressed in the sub-title 'Architecture as science' in Chapter 3.

The titles contain all central terms of the first phase of Rossi's theoretical work. With this text, Rossi provided a precise basis for an architectural urban analysis, which he declared to be an instrument for architectural design. Rossi thereby generated spatial knowledge that is made available for sustainability. He discusses this in his book "Scientific autobiography" as follows: "Around 1960, I wrote "The architecture of the city", a book that was successful. At the time, I was not yet 30 and, as already mentioned, I had intended to write a definitive book. It seemed to me as though everything were clear and fixed… I read books on urban geography, topography and urban history like a general who wishes to know all the possible battlefields: the elevations, the passes, the forests. I went through the cities of Europe, on foot, to grasp their arrangement and classify them into types. As if in an egoistically experienced love, I often overlooked their secret feelings: the system that governed them was sufficient for me."[13]

At the same time, he aimed to maintain the freedom of design within the postulated autonomy of architecture. His method is therefore never binding: Instead, personal sentiments can resist the strictures of method: "Thinking of this mode, I realise that I am especially interested in things that are there to express themselves and the mechanism with which they are able to do so, knowing that another dark mechanism prevents the normal process of operations that would be required for something to happen. That is a

[10] Carlo Aymonino, important Italian architect, urban planner and architectural theorist, born 1926. He is regarded as a representative of rational architecture in Italy.

[11] Ernesto Nathan Rogers, important Italian architect, publisher and teacher. Born 1909, died 1969. Co-owner of the BBPR office, important representative of the Razionalismo.

[12] Rossi 1966

[13] Rossi 1988, p. 30f

Residential estate design in the Gallaratese quarter. Milan 1969–1970. Portico design sketch. In: Rossi 2001, p. 47

part of the problem of freedom; for me, that freedom also fulfils itself in my work. I do not know exactly what kind of freedom it is, but I have found ways of maintaining it."[14]

Design

In a first phase that was characterised by the "Architecture of the city" and also by a purism derived from Italian Rationalism, Rossi's projects were highly abstracted and reduced to basic geometric forms. This especially applies to the monuments that are significant for his early work, such as the San Cataldo cemetery in Modena (1971–1984) and the competition project for the "Resistenza" in Cuneo (1962). By contrast, the designs for apartment projects of the time have a primarily typological orientation, such as the residential estate in Galaratese (1969–1973) or the designs for the villa in Borgo. The theoretical aspects of the "Architecture of the city" are reflected in the main themes of Rossi's architectural work: Typology, permanence, monuments and collective memory, whereby here the aspect of alienation in the sense of a contemporary re-shaping of historical references also contributed to his method.

The second phase – scientific autobiography

In his *Scientific autobiography*, which appeared almost twenty years later, Aldo Rossi provided insight into his handling of architecture and explains how especially his design approach had changed since the publication of the first text. In view of the clear paradigm shift, his own statements in the later work are very direct in shedding light on his handling of knowledge and experience in architectural work.

Rossi's 'Architectural autobiography' impressively documents the transformation towards the architect's later work and explains his method of analogy, which had a decisive effect on his later teaching work. The inclusion of the world of personal sentiment as a component that determines a design forms the basis, before using the method of analogy to establish an unsentimental sobriety. This decisive methodological change is supported by the following quotes from Rossi: "Perhaps this alone would be the design, where analo-

"The analogous city", 1976. Tablet for the Biennale in Venice. In: Rossi 2001, p. 72

gies, identifying oneself with things, become silent again. [...] The design follows this network of connections, memories, images – knowing that it will have to formulate a solution of some kind by the end. On the other hand, the original, true or apparent will be a dark object that is identical to the copy."[15]

"Without wishing to go beyond the limits of science, I must admit that my decisive association was the sound of the hotel name, the green and especially a girl called Rosanna or Rossana. I have never been able to decipher this very individual feeling of paint and opposing colours: the feeling of the noxious green and the rosy Rosanna, between skin colour and a rather unusual flower that unfolded in my image of Sirena."[16]

Rossi increasingly incorporated such analogies into his design work.[17] He describes the development as follows: "I think that both aspects are very important for me and have achieved greater clarity. There is a close relationship between my first attempt to give the field of architecture another foundation and the final result of dissolving or forgetting. [...] To show architecture in its true nature means facing the problem in a scientific way and cleansing it of all superstructure, any emphasis and rhetoric that gathered in the years of the avant garde. It therefore means to increasingly dissolve a myth and place architecture back between visual art and the art of an engineer. [...] It also means that the general conditions must be lived out personally, in small things, since the bigger things, from a historical perspective, have been completed."[18]

The design work of Rossi's third phase, after the publication of his "Scientific autobiography" is therefore an act of self-citation. His late projects became a reproduction of his own formal preconditions from the second phase. His buildings for the IBA Berlin are especially good examples, along with a wide range of other projects outside Italy.

Implementation

The buildings' implementation basically follows the assumptions of the design. In the first phase it was characterised by an abstract purism derived from Razionalismo, the second phase is strongly

[15] Rossi 1988, p. 57
[16] Rossi 1988, p. 44
[17] Rossi 1988, p. 149f
[18] Rossi 1988, p. 149f

San Cataldo Cemetery, Modena 1971–1978. Game of the Goose. In: Rossi 2001, p. 52

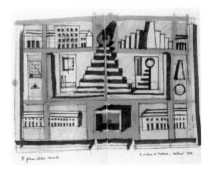

San Cataldo Cemetery, Modena, 1971–1978. Stylised plan, composition with various ground plans and elevations. In: Becker 2003, p. 122

[19] Magnago Lampugnani, Vittorio, "Die Architektur der Stadt als poetische Wissenschaft", in: Becker 2003, p. 53
[20] Herzog und De Meuron in: Werk, Bauen + Wohnen, 12 1997, p. 41

determined by sentiment with reference to materials and colours, while the third phase, as shown above, focuses on the radical continuation of the second phase.

Vittorio Magnago Lampugnani aptly summarized the interaction between theory and practice, and therefore the significance of implementation in Rossi's work: "But if theory was the main determining factor for Rossi's practice, practice itself had its own effect on his theory. It makes it concrete and visible, but also strengthens and expands it. Not just in the way a theoretical promise is practically fulfilled and gains credibility, but also because much that could only be hinted at verbally becomes recognisable in the constructed work with all the wealth of its implications."[19]

It should also be pointed out that generally the implementation only played a very minor role both for the reception of Rossi's work and for Rossi's own reflection upon it. The different statements by his Swiss "students" at the ETH, which were published in the journal Werk, Bauen + Wohnen following his death, are impressive evidence of this. They can be read as the quintessence of the significance of Rossi's work as an architect and a teacher.

Jacques Herzog and Pierre de Meuron for instance wrote in their article on the 'Advantages of sensuousness': "... because Rossi taught a method that allowed the city to be deciphered as it were, to 'read' the location, typologically decode it and, building upon it, to define a historically legitimate approach to a solution. Naturally that is alluring and convenient, but for a future architect who must find his own way in a changing world – it is deadly."[20]

In 'Images against rhetoric', Eraldo Consolascio and Marie-Claude Bétrix stress: "L'Architettura della città', published in 1966, still has validity and uses today, since Rossi's contribution mainly moves on the level of cognition, memory, analysis. In his stringency, he represents one of the most complete syntheses of urban planning analysis. Even if some themes that are especially interesting to us today, addressing aspects of morphology in the periphery, are not discussed in concrete in the book, the working instruments described by Rossi remain a valuable aid. And going beyond the book itself, his – fundamental – bibliography provides insight into spe-

Design for the resistance monument in Cuneo, 1962, Design sketch for the cross-section. In: Rossi 2001, p. 32

cialist literature that determined his work and also his lecturing."[21] In the article entitled "Four branches", Miroslav Šik refers to the breadth of influences upon Aldo Rossi: "My Rossi tree originally had four green branches: Today, three of them have withered. I freely nurture the fourth. ... Rossi first meant Italianità, something stylish, the scent of the Mediterranean ... Rossi was secondly reason and scientific. The typological and morphological urban analysis during term papers under Mario Campi and later Rossi were replaced by semiology. ... The third branch flourished for exactly four semesters. The time was full of sensuousness, passion and craftsman's humility. Whatever one analysed as a young urban analyst, the result at the end of the term was a 'Rossianic project'. [...] I still partially sit upon the fourth branch to this day. As a student, I heard for the first time from Rossi that all architecture acts before the background of its city and history, measures itself up with traditions or dialectically opposes them, that all urban architecture has its stature, permanences that remain distinctive for centuries. To this day, I feel the call of urban architecture, regardless whether the city has become more heterogeneous and full of contrasts, regardless of the mist in which the speed of the times enveils me. His understanding of the analogy revealed very tight boundaries and, like all of us, was dictated by his preferences. But that in no way makes the term 'città analoga' wrong. ..."[22]

Finally Max Bosshard addressed Rossi's teaching very directly in his article entitled 'Research as invention': "Rossi reacted angrily to the question in which way his theoretical investigations flowed into his projects, or in which projects one could find the theoretical intensions of his literature. He stressed that linear deductions between theory and projects do not exist, but that every design is based on principles (or rules). The transition from analysis to design incorporated the design idea on a didactically structured course by pooling cognition and experience to produce design intentions that are clarified in form. The design idea was in a way a litmus test of the architectural work. We objected to this and discussed it intensely – whereby highly contrasting interpretations were able to remain standing."[23]

[21] Consolascio, Bétrix in: Werk, Bauen + Wohnen, 12 1997, p. 42

Single family home by Mount Pocono, Pennsylvania, 1988. Design sketch. In: Rossi 2001, p. 203

Single family home by Mount Pocono, Pennsylvania, 1988. View. In: Rossi 2001, p. 203

[22] Miroslav Šik provides a reference to another level of influence:
"… Aber eins sei noch offenbart: Ohne Rossi wären keine Jaxon-Kreiden in Umlauf gekommen. Einmal kam er während des Semesters endlich nach Zürich, ich glaube direkt von den USA, trug eine Mickymaus-Uhr und präsentierte uns wunderschöne Zeichnungen mit hellblauer Kreide auf einem hauchdünnen gelblichen Skizzenpapier. Als "brave Rossianer" haben wir bis dahin stets mit der Zahnbürste einen dramatischen Wolkenhimmel gespritzt, und siehe da, der Maestro öffnete neue Wege. Ein paar Jahre später werden mit diesen Jaxon-Kreiden perspektivische Bilder à la Paris – Texas gezeichnet. Aber das ist bereits ein anderes Kapitel…" Šik in: Werk, Bauen+Wohnen, 12 1997, p. 44
[23] Bosshard in: Werk, Bauen + Wohnen, 1/2 1998, p. 43

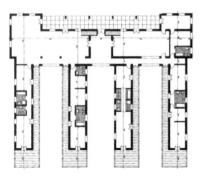

Design for a villa with pavilion in the woods, Borgo Ticinese, 1973. Ground plan and perspective view. In: Rossi 2001, p. 62

The different standpoints of his Swiss "students" impressively highlight the fact that the influence of Aldo Rossi can be especially located on the level of theory and the design method. In view of this influence, it is possible to clearly regard Rossi's paradigm shift as directly connected with the publication of his second book. The same applies to his design method. In the first phase, typological design is of central significance. It is replaced by an analogous approach in the second phase. What was able to exist in a chronological order in Rossi's work clearly became an either-or decision for his Swiss "students". Despite the apparent contradictions in the theory and design method, the students' fascination for Rossi's method – in addition to his personal nature, which can only be imagined from a distance – has remained.

Cognition/Knowledge

If one regards Rossi's architectural activity in the light of this study, the following cycles are apparent with respect to the question of gained cognition, knowledge and forms of knowledge. In the first phase, the method of urban analysis provides the sought after cognition that is intended to determine the design. However as Bruno Reichlin and Fabio Reinhard have pointed out, despite the dominance of analysis, the design process remains strongly autonomous. While the implemented work reveals important components of the knowledge and experience cycle that is clearly recognisable, this is less virulent in the second phase. With respect to his later work, Rossi refers to the fact that for him, the architectural process is as good as completed with the design, i.e. with the development of the project. Only in Rossi's early work does the cognition from the constructed reality have an influence on subsequent designs. In his first phase, which was so influenced by purism, the cognition from the implemented projects, especially with reference to the question of abstraction, is important and subsequently leads to a very intense examination of communicating a mood intended by Rossi, which is characterised by materials and colour. This aspect remains as a fixed component in Rossi's method of analogy.

In the first phase based on the principles of his "Architecture of the city", Rossi uses a precisely postulated proactive theory that can be directly implemented in the design process. However he discovers in the design process that personal experience is somehow always at odds with this concept. He thereby achieves cognition even in the design stage, which occasionally contradicts his theoretical/personal principles. At the same time, the discussion leads to cognition that also influences formal language. It expresses itself clearly in Rossi's preference for pure geometric figures as basic architectural elements, in a reference to Boullée.

In the second phase, Aldo Rossi develops his method of analogy, which continues to uphold the idea of a collective consciousness, as described in the "Architecture of the city", but also addresses the architect's own biographical past as a component of design. This close relationship between personal biography and design work, which can be summarized in the term analogy, is taken up not only by Fabio Reinhart, one of his early companions, but also by Rossi's Zurich students, especially Miroslav Šik, initially in collaboration with Fabio Reinhart, radically incorporating it into their teaching, although Šik seeks the "images" elsewhere in the city compared to Rossi. In this sense, Aldo Rossi's analogous design method in his later period enriches his theoretical structure, which was initially limited to a purely analytical component.

Rossi's initial method of urban analysis and the later developed method of analogy in the design process – as well as possible mixed forms – found continuation in the work of his Swiss students. Interestingly, almost all his successors have detached themselves from his formal preferences and chosen method as a basis for their own work.

Teatro del Mondo, Venice 1979. Design sketches. In: Rossi 2001, p. 88

Venice 1979. The Teatro del Mondo on a section of the Zattere quay. In: Rossi 2001, p. 89

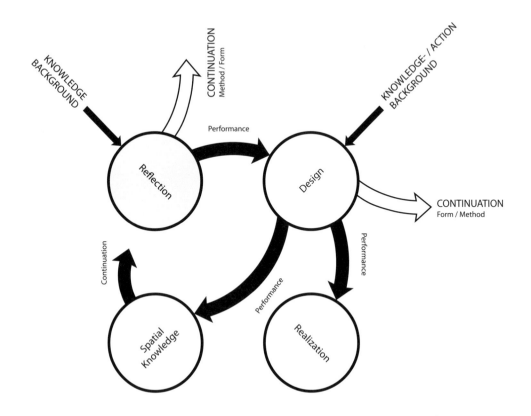

Creative cycle Peter Eisenman

Knowledge background
– Reflection on philosophy, theory of
  literature and linguistics
– PhD
– "Crisis of architecture"
– Publications

Reflection
– Proactive theory
– Teaching
– Articles/books

Continuation
– Style
– References/vocabulary

Knowledge-/action background
– Methods

Design
– Diagrams– Models– 3D

Continuation
– Methods
– Forms

Peter Eisenman
(*1932)

Reflection (proactive theory)

The American architect Peter Eisenman has influenced the archi-tectural scene for more the 50 years and has had a great impact, not only through his few projects that were actually built, such as the Holocaust Memorial in Berlin (2005) and the Wexner Center for the Arts in Columbus in Ohio (1989), but also through his un-implemented designs, his countless articles and books – which far exceed the number of his projects – and his many years of activ-ity in teaching, which have had an effect of several generations of architects.

One can say that the central thought behind Eisenman's work is the question of the reciprocal relationship between theory and practice. He himself describes it as follows (with respect to Peter and Alison Smithson): "For me they represent the essence of what it is to be an architect: a commitment to a set of ideas – a philo-sophical position – and a body of work generated by, represen-tative of, and embodying these ideas."[1] Eisenman was one of the first architects to write a doctoral thesis, in Cambridge, England, in Philosophy, since at the time it was still impossible to write a doctorate in Architecture. It is evidence of his early interest in theo-retical matters.

Eisenman justifies his reference to a theory outside architecture – in his case including philosophy, linguistics and literature – by stating that certain ideas – especially those of intellectual Mod-ernism – have not yet found their way into architecture. Eisenman describes the circumstance he criticises as the "metaphysics of the present", "Classicism" or "Humanism". References to both Jacques Derrida and Michel Foucault are an indication of Eisenman's eclec-ticism, which is discussed below.

Eisenman formulates this criticism for the first time in connection with his early house projects, the *Cardboard Houses*. He uses them to demonstrate how the upheavals in intellectual Modernism have

[1] Eisenman 1971, p. 80

Peter Eisenman: Diagram, diaries. Cover. 1999

[2] Eisenman 1988, p. 7

[3] Gerber, Andri, *Interview Peter Eisenman*, 5. 12. 2003, unpublished

[4] Eisenman states this himself: "Quoi qu'il en soit, il est sans doute également honnête de dire – si je regarde en arrière, jusqu'à ma thèse en 1963 – que j'ai toujours suivi une idée de base, une même ligne qui s'est développée logiquement sur une période de 20 ans et qui n'a pas changé beaucoup. Cette idée de base qui sous-tend mon travail, est la recherche de la consistance de ce que l'on fait lorsque l'on projette et selon la manière dont on le fait." Latour 1977, p. 73

[5] Gerber, Andri, *Interview Peter Eisenman*, New York, 5. 12. 2003, unpublished

[6] "He's always hiding, hiding behind this web – web is a good word, isn't it? Marvelous word, web. He doesn't really understand Nietzsche. He doesn't understand most of the stuff he spouts. He really is the most tremendous bullshitter. But, and here's the point, he's better than a theorist. He's an artist. But he requires theory to make his art, just like Mies required technology, and Hannes Meyer required the proletariat. It's terribly hard to do design. We all need our crutches. And Peter's is his mind." Philipp Johnson, quoted in: Seabrook 1991, p. 127

[7] "E proprio istituendo in una ossessiva autoanalisi di un processo di formalizzazione il fondamento del proprio procedere, Eisenman finisce con lo scambiare per una teoria la pura e semplice ‹descrivibilità› di un percorso progettuale. Ma non è questo il punto più importante. Questa ostinazione a giustificarsi che sa più di razionalismo freudiano che di razionalità architettonica è il limite che trattiene Eisenman al di qua del vero arbitrio oltre il quale avrebbe in realtà senso la sua predicazione." Purini 1987, p. 36

not yet found their way into architecture: "This is because architecture has never had an appropriate theory of Modernism understood to be a set of ideas which deals with the intrinsic uncertainty and alienation of the modern condition."[2]

Eisenman decided to take on the task of making good this "backlog" in architecture and urban planning.

His work can basically be split into three phases: The first lasted from approx. 1963 to 1978, when he was especially influenced by Russian Formalism, Structuralism, the generative grammar of Noam Chomsky and *conceptual* and *minimal art*. The second, which lasted from 1978 to around 1986, focused on the Post-Structuralism of Derrida and the literature of American Post-Modernism, and was characterised by the term "text". The third, still continuing phase is dominated by "blurring", folding, organic forms and a distinction between indented and flat spaces. The most important theoretical influences of the third phase are Gilles Deleuze and Maurice Blanchot[3] and it is this period that we focus upon in this text.

Eisenman builds his work upon a constant extension of certain underlying principles, which are continuously enriched by new concepts and theories.[4] Older concepts and processes are dropped or adapted to accommodate the newer influences. The terms used are "affect", "archaeology", "trace", "aura", "syntax", "strong and weak form", "dislocation", "decomposition", "blurring", "in-between", "graft", "text", "writing", "author", "indexical" etc. Discussion of his work and the accompanying theory is accordingly difficult. His work is also characterised by a very deliberate use of media and his own self-presentation. He announced, carried through and denied the above mentioned paradigm shifts in very theatrical ways.

Despite the apparent lack of stringency and his frequent paradigm shifts, a clear thread can be seen running through Eisenman's entire work. It addresses the relationship between theory and form, the question of implementing an idea in its appropriate form, and consequently a criticism of mimetic presentation. Eisenman regarded *mimesis* in its simplest form, as copying.

In view of the complexity of the theoretical principles upon which Eisenman bases his work, the question of the method with which to approach his work arises. His work, somewhere between written expression and design, seems to simultaneously parry and challenge any criticism. The multilayered theory with which he accompanies his work should be regarded as a challenge to highlight or investigate more deeply any aspect that he himself has only touched upon. Eisenman himself is very aware of the advantages of such an "open" theory and strongly supports any study – as long as it conforms with his intentions – because it enlarges the field of possible interpretation, while also veiling his true intention even more strongly. He himself stresses the fact that his work is determined by different, overlapping influences: "There are lots of things that twist in, there is not only Derrida; that gets mixed together with things."[5]

So he bases his work on a theoretical syncretism that makes it difficult to detect which influence is absorbed and processed in what way. So the more important question is: What role does this theory play in his work? Philipp Johnson, who was very close to Eisenman, states that theory was no more than a necessary "crutch" for designing, and could have been something else.[6] Various Eisenman critics have expressed a similar notion, such as Franco Purini, Pippo Ciorra and Ulrich Schwarz. Purini suggests that Eisenman confuses pure theory with a simple description of the design process.[7] His texts are nothing other than "poetics" of the inexplicable.[8] Ciorra also detects a blurring between theory and poetics in Eisenman's texts, which – according to his hypothesis – he deliberately produces.[9] Ulrich Schwarz stresses that Eisenman's text "is not an autonomous volume of thought" and is constantly moving. Eisenman's working process is experimental and in continuous development, which requires a free approach to borrowed theories.[10] The theory is therefore a changeable instrument and by no means a fixed background that requires adherence. It is simultaneously an instrument and guidance. Eisenman himself repeatedly stresses that he is an architect, not a theoretician; a statement that is calculated and creates further confusion.[11] One comment he made on a book by the Smithsons could serve as an *incipit* of his own work: "It is a book to be enjoyed for its spirit rather than to be admired for its precision."[12] The same could

[8] "Eccessivamente e ossessivamente intelligenti i suoi saggi non riescono ad essere considerati in questo contesto per quello che sono, vale a dire enunciazioni di poetiche calate in una forma saggistica. La poetica eisenmaniana dell'incomunicabilità come volontà di non confrontarsi, può essere da lui enunciata solo attraverso un travestimento che la oggettivizzi e in realtà la neutralizzi sottraendole quella sostanziale aggressività che ne costituisce il segno. Poetica enunciata ma non riconosciuta questo smarrimento nella solitudine e nell'ostilità costituisce senza dubbio uno dei momenti più intensi dell'attuale condizione umana per come questa é rappresentabile." Purini 1987, p. 36

[9] "Sarebbe quindi sbagliato sostenere che nel lavoro di Eisenman il progetto sia subordinato alla formulazione critica o viceversa. É vero piuttosto che Eisenman, come notano molti commentatori, nutre la propria costruzione teorica di una conscia e voluta ambiguità tra poetica e fondamento teorico, tra descrizione di un processo creativo individuale e definizione di codici (de)compositivi generalizzabili. Il legame labile tra le affermazioni teoriche e i progetti ricorda d'altronde la prosa profetica e convincente dei primi maestri del moderno: (...)." Ciorra, Pippo, "Architettura come pretesto", in: Ciorra 1995, p. 21–22

[10] Schwarz 1995, p. 34

[11] "First, I am an architect, not a theoretician or historian, I believe in the inseparability of ideas and form." Eisenman 1973, S. 17

[12] Eisenman 1971, p. 76

[13] Eisenman 1987, S. 5

apply to most of his theoretical statements. Elsewhere he underlines how his essays are a means for invention and not description: "The essays were concurrent and covalent; I could no longer distinguish an analytic activity from a synthetic one in my work. The texts were tools of invention rather than explanation, views of what might happen rather than what had happened."[13] So writing is an essential part of the design process and is a form of action. Together with the designs and projects, the texts form a unit of analytical and synthetic activity that is almost impossible to disentangle. So "theory" and "design" are extremely close to each other. The theory is both a guide to design and a reflection upon that design, thereby forming its framework. It is however neither a direct guide nor a description of the design process, since it is too abstract.

Peter Eisenman: Diagram, diaries.
Overview diagram. In: Eisenman 1999

Design

In view of these conditions and the complexity of Eisenman's work, this study is limited to a short, relatively manageable phase of his work, namely "folding". Eisenman's main explanation of the concept of folding can be found in a text he wrote in 1991, "Unfolding Events: Frankfurt Rebstock and the possibility of a new urbanism", which acted as an accompanying text for his competition entry for the Rebstock park project in Frankfurt. In the text, Eisenman includes an observation on the significance and effect of the media, including "events" such as rock concerts, upon society and its spaces. In the same text, he also describes urban planning to date as a static affair that is incompatible with the nature of such "events". Hitherto, urban planning was determined by a clear relationship between *Figure* and *Ground*, or by the Modernist *tabula rasa*. Eisenman postulates his folding concept in opposition to such a perspective and refers to the work of the French philosopher Gilles Deleuze – or more precisely his book *Le Pli – Leibniz et le baroque*, which was written in 1988 and published in English in 1993 – as well as the disaster theory by the mathematician René Thom, without explicitly quoting any of his work. Folding in urban planning should be regarded as a process rather than a static object. It creates a condition of "displacements", "blurring"[14] and a hybrid

Peter Eisenman: Model, Haus Immendorff, 1993. In: Eisenman 2003

of *figure* and *ground*.[15] Folding means an event both in its process and in the result. Eisenman describes such urban planning as "weak urbanism". His aim was to overcome the unidimensionalism of his previous work, which predominantly consisted of extruding over-lapping structures.

The design for the Rebstock park project consists of extensive computer and cardboard models that, starting with standard hous-ing blocks and the existing topography, are folded into "fractal for-mations". The design work therefore comprises countless studies and models that "experiment" with various different configurations. It is impossible to discover which parameters – other than formal and aesthetic ones – these models must fulfil. The diagram also plays a major role since it simultaneously presents and changes: "As a generative device in a process of design, the diagram is also a form of representation. But unlike traditional forms of repre-sentation, the diagram is a generator is a mediation between a pal-pable object, a real building, and what can be called architecture's interiority."[16] It is also located between word and form.[17]

In addition to the Rebstock park – which is regarded as paradig-matic for the folding phase – this process was also applied to other projects, such as the implemented *Nunotani Headquarters in Tokyo* (1991, already demolished) and the *Aronoff Center for Design and Art, University of Cinncinnati* (1996). The theory of folding is im-plemented very directly. The principle is both theory and method ("folding").

Implementation

In connection with the *Cardboard Houses* alone, it is clear that im-plementation represents no additional cognition, even that imple-mentation is irrelevant because many of its presentations do not survive the implementation.

In the case of *Cardboard Houses*, the buildings should resemble models as much as possible (hence the description "Cardboard"). Only a few of the implemented designs could withstand the test of time and even then only through intensive restoration. The Wexner Center also had to be almost completely renovated only a few years after its erection. And one of his last projects, the cul-

[14] "In such a displacement, the new, rather than being understood as fundamentally different to the old, is seen instead as being merely slightly out-of-focus in re-lation to what exists. This out-of-foc us condition then, has the possibility of blurring or displacing the whole, that is both old and new. One such displacement possibility can be found in the form of the fold." Eisenman 1993, p. 60

[15] "The fold in this sense is neither figure nor ground but contains aspects of both." Eisenman 1993, p. 61

[16] Eisenman 1999, p. 27

[17] "As the dominant device within the hybrid practices of the architect-critics of the neo-avant-garde, this more specific use of the diagram promises to elide Rowe's postwar oppositions between physique-form and morale-word. Where-as Rowe would elevate the former pair over the latter in his attempt to extend the legacy of modernism (in contrast to his alter ego, Banham, who would elab-orate the implications of the second pair), the architects of the neo-avantgarde are drawn to the diagram because – unlike drawing or text, partis pris or bubble notation – it appears in the first instance to operate precisely between form and word." Somol, R.E., "Dummy Text, or The Diagrammatic Basis of Contemporary Architecture" in: Eisenman 1999, p. 8

18 "Conversation with Peter Eisenman", in: Bédard 1994, p. 123

tural centre in Santiago de Compostela (1999–), is also revealing, as complex geometries could only be implemented using elaborate hanging boards that appear to have no relationship to the ceiling.

Spatial knowledge

The question of the importance of theory lies at the heart of the question of cognition/knowledge for the architect. Is Eisenman's handling deliberate and objective – which could be assumed in view of the *quantity* of his theory – or is it subjective, making his theory aleatory and uncontrolled? Eisenman himself flirted with the question: "I can honestly tell you that most of my work is unconscious. Most of the time the discoveries are made in the misreading of something else. I never read Deleuze on folding until after the fact."[18] One may doubt the truth of this statement. Yet it is impossible to judge whether the theory and the models are only instruments of design or whether they represent their legitimacy and are deliberately deployed. But as Johnson expressed above, one can nevertheless state that theory is part of his design. Eisenman only achieves new forms by writing texts, by addressing certain influences and by declaring his own "architectural philosophy". The cognition gained through theory/observation is analogous to a metacompetence in handling such theories and their integration into his own design work, even though the constant paradigm shifts are also a sign of the uncontrollability of the process. Design can nevertheless be regarded as a form of implementing a particular theory. It is revealed in the experimental character of his projects and his work on countless models. Only by experimenting with (virtual and real) models and diagrams does Eisenman find a valid implementation of his theory. Diagrams play an especially important role – albeit less so in connection with folding – in developing a method of design from a theory.

Eisenman's design work can be described as research because spatial knowledge is created with respect to the actual question that drives him, namely the relationship between form and content. The fact that Eisenman repeatedly introduced paradigm shifts into his work should be regarded as an attempt to shed light on this relationship

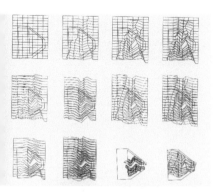

Peter Eisenman: Church of the Year 2000. Diagram. In: Eisenman 2003

from various perspectives. Eisenman's intention lies in the translation of specific outlooks and world views. That is why he continues to work on his instruments, especially his diagrams, models and computer models. Despite or perhaps because of the complexity of his theory, with its great visual quality, the sustainability of this knowledge is marked by a permanent questioning of the instruments and methods that serve his work.

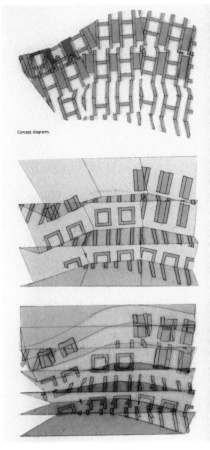

Concept diagrams.

Peter Eisenman: Rebstockpark, Master Plan, 1990–1991. In: Davidson (Ed.) 2006

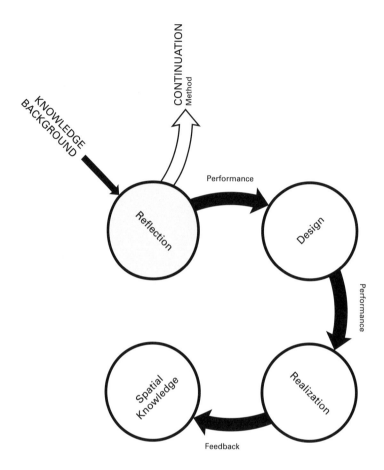

Creative cycle
Christopher Alexander

Knowledge background
– Studies in mathematics
– PhD

Reflection
– Proactive theory
– Form as problem
– Teaching in Berkeley

Continuation
– Diagrams
– Patterns

Christopher Alexander
(*1936)

Proactive theory

Born in Austria in 1936, Alexander fled with his parents, who were both archaeologists, to England after the Anschluss. He first studied Mathematics and then Architecture in Cambridge. He recalls he wanted to study architecture from the outset, but was forced to learn a "serious" profession first. The Architecture course proved to be a great challenge for him because he found it too aleatory owing to his scientific background.[1] After graduating, he went to Harvard in the USA and worked on a dissertation for the newly established doctorate programme in Architecture, one of the first in the USA. His dissertation was published in 1964 with the title *Notes on the Synthesis of Form*. The book became the "founding text of a movement that attempted to bring mathematical and scientific methods to architectural design."[2] At the same time, Alexander worked at MIT, which was then one of the leading Architecture faculties that focused on the use of computers in architecture. In this respect, Alexander and a colleague Marvin Manheim undertook initial attempts to apply his systems using a computer.[3] He also worked at the *Center for Cognitive Studies* in Harvard together with Jerome Bruner.[4] In 1963 he moved to the University of California, Berkeley, where he remained until his retirement and still lives today. In 1967, he founded the *Center for Environmental Structure* there, where he continued his research and work.

His mathematical training and his experience in handling mathematical tasks and solutions characterise Alexander's *background knowledge*, which determined his perspective on architecture.[5] For him, the aim was to prove his process. In addition to Alexander, Nicolas Negroponte at MIT and the group led by Lionel March in Cambridge should also be mentioned, since they encouraged comparable studies and were also trained as architects.

Due to his mathematical background knowledge, Alexander devel-

[1] "I was simply shocked. Here I was, still young, swimming up to my neck in mathematics, quite challenged, but able to hold my own. Then I get into this program and it was quite clear to me that it did not make sense on any level. I was asked to do incredible and absurd things which did not relate to each other or even make sense individually. I was lost and became quite angry – but also quite panicked." Aus: Grabow, Alexander 1983, p. 30

[2] Keller 2007, p. 157

[3] Alexander, Manheim 1962

[4] Grabow, Alexander 1983, p. 51

[5] "As you know, I studied mathematics for a long time. What I learned, among other things, was that if you want to specify something precisely, the only way to specify it and be sure that you aren't kidding yourself, is to specify a clearly defined step-by-step process which anyone can carry out, for constructing the thing you are trying to specify. In short, if you really understand what a fine piece of architecture is – really, thoroughly understand it – you will be able to specify a step-by-step process which will always lead to the creation of such a thing." in: Jacobson 1971, p. 768

"Writing Notes on the Synthesis of Form, Cambridge, Mass 1960."
In: Grabow 1983

[6] "Problems have outgrown a single individual's capacity to handle them. Society must invent ways and means that, in effect, magnify the designer's limited capacity and make it possible for him to apply himself more completely to those problems that he is well equipped to solve." Chermayeff, Alexander 1965, p. 109–110

[7] "On the other hand, 'A new theory of urban design' really does describe what we have. We have a formulation of an entirely new way of looking at urban design, together with a detailed experiment which shows, in part, what this new theory can do." Alexander, Christopher, Neis, Anninou, King 1987, p. 2

[8] Chermayeff, Alexander 1965, p. 53

[9] "There is an important working principle to note at the outset: Every problem has a structural pattern of its own. Good design depends on the designer's ability to act according to this structure and not to run arbitrarily counter to it." Chermayeff, Alexander 1965, p. 152–153

[10] "Each pattern describes a problem which occurs over and over again in our environment, and then describes the core of the solution to that problem, in such a way that you can use this solution a million times over, without ever doing it the same way twice." Alexander, Ishikawa, Silverstein 1977, p. 10

[11] "Each pattern is a rule which describes what you have to do to generate the entity which it defines." Alexander 1979, p. 182

oped the perception that architecture is a highly complex problem that can no longer be solved by a purely intuitive process.[6]

He based his *theory* – and he explicitly speaks on several occasions of a theory in the sense of a design guide[7] – on the premise that systems – regardless whether they are a teapot or a city, to name two examples used by Alexander, can be reduced to sub-systems or so-called *patterns* (the term is first used in 1963)[8]. He initially presented them as *trees* and then as *lattices*, diagrams he derived from the field of mathematics. In some places he also called the systems "sets". Patterns – that can only inadequately be translated into the German "Muster" – are the structures existing within an object, with which the designer must accord.[9] They are the description of a problem[10] as well as a law that explains how a whole can be created from a *pattern*.[11] He thereby attempted to present complex systems and make them comprehensible.

The re-combining of partial systems should then be carried out entirely intuitively, although it is determined by the choice of connections and the framework of the system. But this is precisely where Alexander was unable to describe how the process of synthesis functions. So his book should really be called the *analysis*, rather than *synthesis*, of form, as he himself partially admits.[12]

Alexander developed this theory ever further, but he thereby increasingly distanced himself from the mechanistic positivism of his first phase, which was mainly characterised by attempts to implement his theory using computer programs. He himself later stressed that they no longer felt convincing to him. With hindsight, Alexander describes his work as the search for beauty and the possibilities of creating beauty.

Within his work Alexander repeatedly addressed the relationship between art and science, whereby he attacked everything coincidental and aleatory as unacceptable, without making his position really clear. He associated the relationship between art and science with intuition and rational predetermination, without explaining how he regarded the ideal nature of such a relationship to be. The aim of his work was the reunification of art and science, leading to a new Humanism. Although in his early work he clearly expressed the necessity of rational perception of what had hitherto remained intuitive,[13] he later preferred the subjective aspect in a second phase, which should unfold within the *pattern* system determined by him. So while he began by aspiring for the "scientification" of architecture, his opinion changed with time until he instead spoke of the "architecturalisation" of science. But until the end, Alexander kept his scientific vocabulary, speaking of *theory, simulation* and *experiment*.

At the time, Alexander's work was regarded as revolutionary and attracted great attention. He is seen as the father of the *Design Method*, but critical voices were quick to react, pointing out the system's insufficiency and lack of logic. So even architects who tried to apply the system used critical words with respect to its stringency and applicability, especially concerning the question of a synthesis.[14]

Many people described his work as "pseudo-science".[15] Even the scientific camp deemed Alexander's theories to be unsound.[16] He was accused of having turned away from the radicality of his earlier research and the reason for this was quickly attributed to his new environment in California, as can be seen for instance in the essay with the telling title "Californian regression or the factualisation of myth" ("kalifornische Regression oder die Versachlichung des

[12] "Finding the right design program or a given problem is the first phase of the design process. It is, if we like, the analytical phase of the process. This first phase of the process must of course be followed by the synthetic phase, in which a form is derived from the program. We shall call this synthetic phase *the realization of the program*. Although these notes are given principally to the analytical phase of the process, and to the invention of programs which can make the synthesis of form a reasonable task, we must no spend a little time thinking about the way this synthesis or realization will work. Until we do so, we cannot know how to develop the details of the program." Alexander 1964, p. 84

[13] "The use of logical structures to represent design problems has an important consequence. It brings with it the loss of innocence. A logical picture is easier to criticize than a vague picture since the assumptions it is based on are brought out into the open. Its increased precision gives us the chance to sharpen our conception of what the design process involves. But once what we do intuitively can be described and compared with nonintuitive ways of doing the same things, we cannot go on accepting the intuitive method innocently." Alexander, Christopher, 1964, p. 8–9

[14] "Individual patterns must be brought together, somehow or other, into design for buildings. Clearly, combinations are always theoretically possible, but it is difficult to understand the practical mechanism of the combinatorial process. Once understood, the use of the patterns would be open to those who would not ordinarily claim to be designers, and perhaps even to machines." Duffy, Torrey, 1970, p. 265

[15] "Poser des conditions, ni contrôlables, ni vérifiées, a tout l'air d'un duperie pseudo-scientifique destinée à l'impressionner le profane." Dreyfus 1971, p. 145

[16] "To a professional philosopher much of his presentation seems grotesquely, and rather dangerously, naïve and confused. I realize of course, that Alexander is not a philosopher and that it would not be just to hold him responsible for knowledge of the more sophisticated subtleties of a discipline which is not his own." Daley, p. 74

[17] "La régression californienne ou la réification du mythe, Christopher Alexander, une Conférence", AMC 38, 1976, p. 76–77

[18] "Obviously the intent is to create well-defined procedures which will enable people to design better buildings. The odd thing is that in the vast proportion of the literature people have lost sight completely of this objective. For instance, the people who are messing around with computers have obviously become interested in some kind of toy. They have very definitely lost the motivation for making better buildings. I feel a terrific part of it has become an intellectual game, and it's largely for that reason that I've dissociated myself from the field." Jacobson 1971, p. 768

[19] Jacobson 1971, p. 768

[20] "The fact is that is that it has solved very few problems for me in my design work. Most of the difficulties of design are not of the computable sort." Jacobson 1971, p. 768

[21] "A propos de la validation de l''analogie linguistique', nous avions constaté que les indices d'une similitude entre le 'pattern langage' et une langue naturelle étaient minces." Arnold 1977, p. 77

Mythos").[17] It discusses the unadapted nature of the results and the relative uselessness of his methods, but in the context of the potential wealth of his approach. Alexander himself explained his increasing disinterest in computers and programming by the fact that it seemed to him to have become a toy, which distracted him from the essential aspect of designing better buildings.[18] In the same interview, he stresses that his interest in *design methodology* is justified by the current "condition" of architecture, but also that it meant an escape from the creative moment of design.[19] It was therefore not of great assistance to him.[20] At a later date, Alexander explained the *patterns* in connection with language and genetics. But such analogies do not contribute much to a better understanding of *patterns*. On the contrary, they strengthen the accusation of being unscientific and imprecise.[21]

Despite the widespread criticism, it should be noted how his theory of *patterns* influenced an entire field of computer programming, which still refers back to him today.[22]

Alexander's theories have been repeatedly discussed in architectural theory, especially with respect to the question of the potential of parametric design and genetic emergence. One example is the issue of Arch+ that was published in October 2008 and is dedicated to the subject of patterns.[23]

Design

The various above-mentioned criticisms regarding the inconsistency of Alexander's theory are also confirmed in his inability to derive a design from it. He worked on several large and small-scale projects and also implemented some of them, but it is unclear how his language of *patterns* is meant to work, or what is different about it compared to a normal design process. His projects, for instance for the Café Linz in Austria, appear to be classical reminiscences, as Georges Teyssot correctly recognised.[24] Alexander defends himself against such statements by pointing out that his architecture incorporates universal laws.

In the first phase of his work, Alexander especially used diagrams as a design instrument. In the description of *Hidecs 2*, the computer program he developed together with Marvin Manheim at MIT, the terms *graphs* and *tree* are used for the first time. They are two forms of diagram with which Alexander attempted to demonstrate the problem.[25] In principle, he states it is only a matter of "requirements" and "interaction between requirements". He continued to develop the diagram ever further until he almost completely turned his back on it. It is clear that it can only describe the analysis and decomposition of parts of the system. The diagram stems from mathematics. He distinguished between three types of diagram, "form", "requirement" and "constructive" diagrams, the last of which was being preferred.

The question of the elements with which Alexander aimed to implement his *patterns* is indicative. Initially, the language is only of "form", while later the aim is to implement "space". He repeatedly asks himself the question of the form or space the *patterns* take, without finding a definitive answer.

With reference to form, *patterns* can be objects – "typical arrangement in space of physical objects (or parts)"[26] – geometric and event patterns – "these patterns of events are always interlocked with certain geometric patterns in the space"[27] – with the latter somehow connected to space – "and that the patterns of events are linked, *somehow*, to space"[28] (author's italics) – and morphological laws – "Each of these patterns is a morphological law, which establishes a set of relationships in space".[29] A transformation begins around 1979. Instead of form, space is focused upon. *Patterns* are then operators that create differences in space - "Each pattern is an operator which differentiates space: that is, it creates distinctions where no distinction was before."[30]

Diagrams are gradually discarded or play only a marginal role, and *patterns* are illustrated using images or drawings.

For example: In *The Oregon Experiment* of 1975, Alexander describes his proposal for the extension of the Oregon University campus. *Patterns* are initially described as a "basis for a shared agreement in the community" and then more precisely as "planning principles". Patterns are reduced to principles here. They are summarized, each described in words and are illustrated using images, plans and/or

[22] "Die Bedeutung von Mustern bei der Erstellung komplexer Systeme wurde schon lange in anderen Disziplinen erkannt. Insbesondere Christopher Alexander und seine Mitarbeiter waren vermutlich die ersten, die Mustersprachen als Mittel zur Konstruktion von Gebäuden und Städten vorgeschlagen haben. Seine Ideen und Beiträge andere Personen haben jetzt in der Objektorientierung Fuss gefasst."
Booch, Grady, "Begleitwort", in: Gamma, Erich et. al. (Ed.), 2004
[23] *Entwurfsmuster*, Arch+ 189, October 2008
[24] "The building has an original, in some ways even neoclassical appearance: at least the 'comfortable' version of neo-classicism, that of K. F. Schinkel's work on a smalls scale, for instance the New Pavilion in the grounds of Charlottenburg Castle (1824–25) or the Swiss 'Chalet' in the Pfaueninsel (1821)." Teyssot, Georges, 1983/IV, p. 72
[25] Alexander, Manheim 1962, p. 3–4
[26] Duffy, Torrey 1970, p. 262
[27] Alexander 1979, p. 75
[28] Alexander 1979, p. 81
[29] Alexander 1979, p. 90
[30] Alexander 1979, p. 373

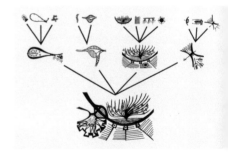

Diagram. In: Alexander 1964

[31] Alexander 1987
[32] Alexander 1975, p.5
[33] Alexander 1975, p. 39
[34] "The fact is, that we have written this book as a first step in the society-wide process by which people will gradually become conscious of their own pattern languages, and work to improve them. We believe, and have explained in The Timeless Way of Building, that the languages which people have today are so brutal, and so fragmented, that most people no longer have any language to speak of at all – and what they do is not based on human, or natural considerations." Alexander, Ishikawa, Silverstein 1977, p. 15–16

diagrams. So in this case, *patterns* express nothing about form and space, which is determined by the patterns' user without a real reference to it.

Alexander also applies *patterns* in his teaching. In *A new theory of urban design* (1987), he reports on a term paper with students in 1978. The paper's aim was to develop the San Francisco storefront. Alexander describes the work as an "experiment" and as a "simulation". Students had to develop 90 projects for the area and achieve organic growth. The "experiment" was only a partial success, since the result was very unsettled, too superficial and some of the building forms were peculiar.[31] If one takes Alexander at his word, it seems the process of *patterns* involves no more than the joint discussion of the process.

So the system of pattern serves to grasp a problem, but also creates an underlying basis for the collaboration in a project. Nevertheless, the basis is insecure since the *patterns* cannot determine the architecture after all, which remains Alexander's intention.

Implementation

The application of *patterns* therefore requires participative design. For Alexander, design is a process that is only successful if a maximum number of people involved in the project also participate in the design process. Accordingly, *patterns* develop into instruments that are meant to be used by all. For instance in the *Oregon Experiment*: "All decisions about what to build, and how to build it, will be in the hands of the users."[32] Furthermore: "It can mean any process by which the users of an environment help to shape it. The most modest kind of participation is the kind where the user helps to shape a building by acting as a client for an architect. The fullest kind of participation is the kind where users actually build their buildings for themselves."[33] In this process, the *patterns* themselves should be improved by all through their general use, underlining Alexander's grassroots political opinions.[34]

Knowledge

Regardless of the question of the extent to which Alexander's theory moved away from his original intentions, it can be said that

Christopher Alexander: Diagram, 1963.
In: Chermayeff, Alexander 1965

he was never able to implement it. His designs in no way represent content that is associated with his *patterns*. They are too vaguely defined and he also fails precisely in the matter of spatial implementation. Implementation leads to a failure that allows no recourse to theory, even if Alexander believed to detect theory in it. Alexander's spatial knowledge exists in his failure, his inability to implement, not least because he originally insisted on a hardly tenable understanding of architecture as a design guide. He does not find the instruments – despite his work on diagrams and patterns – to implement his intentions. Nevertheless, his very failure and his search is inspiration for other architects who wish to take similar paths.

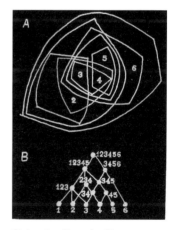

Christopher Alexander: Diagram.
In: Alexander, "The city is not a tree".
In: Architectural Forum 122/1965

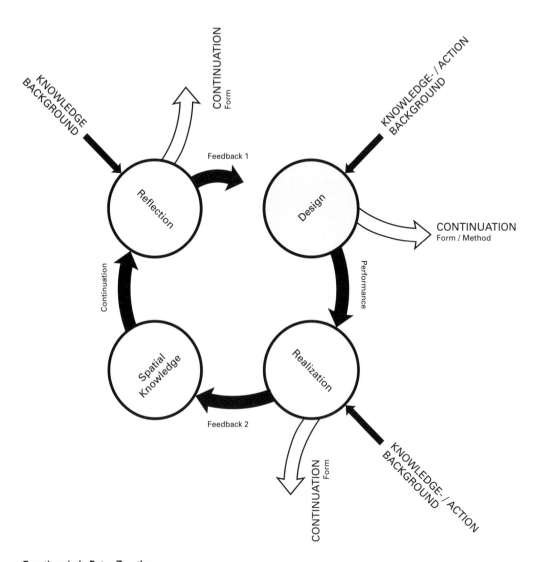

CONTINUATION
Form

KNOWLEDGE
BACKGROUND

KNOWLEDGE- / ACTION
BACKGROUND

Feedback 1

Reflection

Design

CONTINUATION
Form / Method

Continuation

Performance

Spatial
Knowledge

Realization

Feedback 2

CONTINUATION
Form

KNOWLEDGE- / ACTION
BACKGROUND

Creative circle Peter Zumthor

Action-/knowledge background
– Education
– Work in preservation of monuments

Design
– Work with images
– Oversized models
– Sketches

Continuation
– Models
– Sketches
– Reference to context

Realization
– Construction details

Continuation
– Formal emulation

Knowledge background
– Articles and books on design-processes

Reflection
– Reactive theory
– Text/Books

Continuation
– "Poetic style"

Peter Zumthor
(*1943)

Design

The architect Peter Zumthor has a special status on the contemporary architecture scene, not only due to his career, but also through his idiosyncratic, "unfashionable" architecture.[1] Trained as a furniture carpenter in his father's business, he later studied Interior Design at the Basel School of Design and then Architecture at the Pratt Institute in New York. After that, he worked for almost ten years on monumental preservation in Graubünden, before founding his own architectural office in 1979 in Haldenstein near Chur. The point of departure for his work is the design. He does not work with any theory and his work begins directly at the design stage[2], which is determined by images. They are images from the architect's memory; images he allows to evolve in his head while working on the location and the programme: "Images are a means of designing architecture. They are perhaps my primary means and the memory is saved in images."[3] In this context, Zumthor speaks of a "working method".[4] It may seem paradoxical that an architect that has become famous for the sensual nature of his projects should speak of *images*. But these are not the striking images that are well known in commercialised architecture. Instead the images stem from the spirit, yet are concrete rather than abstract.[5] They are not reproductions of forms, but reflect the unique qualities of the content, a context. The images are initially obscure and have there own materialism.[6] The creativity develops out of shaping them. Something is created that did not exist before, something the architect himself could not imagine. Zumthor describes this process as "creating reality".[7] The design process is therefore a process of transformation, from reality to an image, to a memory and from there back to the reality of the project. He describes it as a "process of playful discovery."[8]
Working on reality – Zumthor speaks of the magic of reality – is a decisive aspect. The aim is to create architecture that becomes

[1] Zumthor was awarded the Pritzker Prize in 2009
[2] "Ich beginne nie bei der Theorie, sagt Zumthor, und ich bin eigentlich auch kein guter Beobachter von Architektur. Der Weg eines Entwurfs ist mir bis heute selbst ein letztlich unergründlicher geblieben." Meier 1992, p. 47–48
[3] *Daidalos* 1998, p. 90
[4] *Daidalos* 1998, p. 90
[5] "Und diese inneren Bilder, die nun entstehen, zeigen, weil sie eben Bilder sind, sofort ganz viele Facetten des zu schaffenden Artefaktes. Sie sind ganzheitlich, farbig. Keine Abstraktion, sondern konkret. Sie sind mehr Gefühl als Gedanke. Das Bild, im Gegensatz zum analytischen Gedanken, ist synthetisch, ganzheitlich. Das Bild umfasst viel mehr, als ich zu Beginn verstehe. Erst nach und nach lerne ich, meine Bilder zu verstehen und in einem schlüssigen Entwurf zu ordnen. Aber am Anfang war das Bild." Zumthor 2006, p. 61/63
[6] "Am Anfang ist ein unscharfes Bild, es setzt sich zusammen aus tausend Sinneseindrücken und Absichten und dann wird das immer mehr zu einem Haus, zur Architektur. Das Bild hat von Anfang an seine eigene Materialität, seine eigenen Gesetze, seine eigenen Regeln." *Daidalos* 1998, p. 93
[7] Zumthor 2006 (1), p. 72
[8] Zumthor 1997, p. 11

[9] Zumthor 2006 (1), p. 60
[10] "Dass Gebäude wirkt zuerst als Körper, dort wo es steht, und später als Gedanke, als Bild in den Köpfen der Menschen, die es wahrnehmen. Seine Form zeigt eigene Deutungen der Aufgabe und veranlasst fremde. Architektur schafft und verändert Bilder, real und im Kopf, sie verändert Sehgewohnheiten." Zumthor 2006, p. 69–70
[11] Zumthor 2006 (1), p. 74–75
[12] Archithese 1996, p. 28–36
[13] Zumthor 2007, p. 25
[14] Zumthor 1997, p. 11

Peter Zumthor: Therme Vals, 1996.
Reference image. In: Zumthor 2007

Peter Zumthor: Therme Vals, 1996.
Model photo. In: Zumthor 1997

part of reality, which was initially absorbed in images. The aim is to achieve something that accords with the inner image one has of a location: "Reality impresses me in specific moments. I am moved by an observation. I perceive beauty. And by interaction, an inner image of what I see is created while I am observing it."[9] Design is created from the interaction between the "magic of reality" and the images that inspire it within the designer, as well as the attempt to transform them into reality. Once these images are implemented, they can change not only reality, but also "seeing habits".[10] Zumthor also describes such a reality as bodies and regards himself as a "body surrounded by bodies".[11]

So Zumthor is interested in reality that he observes and absorbs, rather than a theory, or in his own words: "...because as an architect I start with the world I see, experience, roam through, touch and smell, not theories."[12]

Such a handling of the location and the images it evokes can best be explained using Zumthor's project for a spa in Vals (1996). The quality of the project can be seen by the many "pre-images" that Zumthor has combined to produce a harmonious unity: "... the many rockfall and avalanche protection galleries on the road from Ilanz to Vals and the dam on Lake Zevreila further down the valley; all of which are powerful architecture; engineering structures that defy the power of the mountain even inside it and therefore express appropriate strength. And the interior spaces of these constructions always feel significant. Sometimes they resemble cathedrals, as the image from inside the Albigna dam shows."[13] He reduces these images to three elements and a series of procedures related to them: "mountain, stone, water – building in stone, building with stone, building into the mountain."[14] The images serve as the basis for moods and processes of creation – hollowing out. They are not formal example images.

Sketching and modelling are the instruments of the design. Zumthor describes sketching as "playful research work"[15] that, in the case of Vals, serves to study the different compositions of "mass and hollow spaces, opening and condensation, rhythm, repetition and variation."[16] Especially in Vals, the design process unfolds over a large series of sometimes colourful sketches that investigate the different orders and rhythms for the blocks and empty spaces of the spa.

Models also play an important role in the design process. They are mostly built to a very large scale and whenever possible, in the same or a similar material with which the building is then constructed. Its sensual qualities are thereby revealed in advance and tested on the model. A 1:50 model was produced for Vals, "representing the level of the bathing area. The stone cubes are placed in a steel basin filled with water, as blue radiates from all the pools and joints treated with antifreeze. This interior bath model has been exhibited many times throughout the world and photographed for a variety of publications. Despite the later changes, the photographs provide a preview of the spatial atmosphere: stone, light and water reflections, as well as the interplay of colours."[17]

Implementation

Implementing such images in form and space, so that they submit to reality or change it, requires a high level of craftsmanship and technical perfection, which is one of Zumthor's hallmarks. He states that "no idea exists outside of things," revealing his interest in the nature of such things.[18] The aim is "to use an artificial act to create things and yet remove their artificiality, bringing them closer to the everyday world and natural things," as well as "having faith that truth lies in the things themselves."[19] Starting with such work with images, the architecture of Zumthor is an architecture of action, technique, and the manipulation of space and materials.[20]

Working with the stone in Vals stimulates the invention of a new construction technique and the creation of faith in it. The material is called gneiss, which was hitherto only used on roofs in Vals before the spa was built. The material is an instrument of design in the same way as the space or forms. The idea is not superordinate, but is found in the objects themselves – not just their mere appearance, but also what their appearance reveals about their nature.

In addition to the details for the gneiss stone inserted into the concrete in Vals, a table construction was also chosen. It allows the

[15] "Das Zeichnen war spielerische Forschungsarbeit ohne architektonische Vorbilder. Ich erinnere mich an ein Gefühl von grosser Freiheit in der Verfolgung kompositorischer Themen, die wir an Hand dieser Blockstudien entwickelten, in spontanen Zeichnungen zur Form kommen liessen und im Gespräch zu verstehen versuchten." Zumthor 2007, p. 38

[16] Zumthor 2007, p. 38

[17] Hauser, Sigrid, "Entwurf", in: Zumthor 2007, p. 57

[18] "Es ist nicht die Wirklichkeit der von den Dingen abgelösten Theorien, es ist die Wirklichkeit der konkreten Bauaufgabe, die auf dieses Wohnen zielt, die mich interessiert, auf die ich meine Einbildungskraft richten will. Es ist die Wirklichkeit der Baumaterialien – Stein, Tuch, Stahl, Leder… – und die Wirklichkeit der Konstruktionen, die ich verwende um das Bauwerk aufzurichten, in deren Eigenschaften ich mit meiner Vorstellungskraft einzudringen versuche, um Sinn und Sinnlichkeit bemüht, damit vielleicht der Funke des geglückten Bauwerkes zündet, das den Menschen zu behausen vermag. Die Wirklichkeit der Architektur ist das Konkrete, das Form-, Masse- und Raumgewordene, ihr Körper. Es gibt keine Idee, ausser in den Dingen. Das ist der harte Kern der Schönheit." Zumthor 1992, p. 69

[19] Zumthor 1992, p. 69

[20] See: Steinman, Martin, "Techne, Zur Arbeit von Peter Zumthor", in: Zumthor 1988

[21] "Steintische, geschlossene Kavernen und ein grosser Hohlraum zwischen den Tischen, der sich zum Himmel und nach vorne zur Aussicht öffnet – mit diesen Grundelementen ist das räumliche Repertoire des Bades entwickelt. Die Steinbruchbilder des Anfangs haben sich verwandelt und haben begonnen, die Form von architektonischen Konstruktionen und benutzbaren Räumen anzunehmen." Zumthor 2007, p. 43
[22] Meier 1992, p. 47–48
[23] Daidalos 1998, p. 93
[24] "Für Stevens bleibt die Realität das gesuchte Ziel, lese ich weiter im Klappentext des Buches. Der Surrealismus, so wird er zitiert, beeindrucke ihn nicht, denn er erfinde, ohne zu entdecken. 'Eine Muschel Akkordeon spielen zu lassen, heisst erfinden, nicht entdecken', sagt er. Hier erscheint er noch einmal, dieser Grundgedanke, den ich von Williams und Hanke zu kennen glaube und den ich auch aus den Bildern Edward Hoppers herauszuspüren vermeine: Nur zwischen der Wirklichkeit der Dinge und der Imagination zündet der Funke des Kunstwerkes." Zumthor 1992, p. 69
[25] "Also, sagt Peter Zumthor, das Entwerfen sei kein linearer Vorgang, der logisch und schnurgerade auf das Ziel zuführe. Es ist ein von rationalen, zugleich von irrationalen Eingebungen unterbrochener, beförderter, gestörter, beflügelter Prozess und beileibe nicht nur das, was man Kopfarbeit nennt. Entwerfen sei das 'ständige Zusammenspiel von Gefühl und Verstand', und zwar genau in dieser Reihenfolge. Das 'Eigentliche' entstehe durch Emotion und Eingebung oder, etwas salopper gesagt: es kommt aus dem Bauch, dann wird es vom Kopf kontrolliert, 'aufwendig intellektuell' erwogen, verworfen, korrigiert, verbessert, komplettiert. Beim Stichentscheid am Schluss entscheide freilich 'immer wieder der Bauch'." Sack, Manfred, "Über Peter Zumthors Art zu entwerfen, also zu denken", in: Zumthor 1997, p. 75–76

building to appear hollowed out while enabling the ceiling slabs and walls to be separated from each other, letting level light shine in: "Stone tables, closed caverns and a large hollow space between the tables that opens out towards the sky and forwards towards the view: The spa uses these basic elements for its spatial repertoire. The images of a quarry at the start of the project have transformed to assume the form of the architectural construction and usable rooms."[21]

The Vals spa leads to the observation that the mood emanating in the bathing facility is mainly a result of the clear construction and the effect of the details, which the materials and their qualities and interaction create. Zumthor can only implement his intentions by producing sketches, models and details.

Spatial knowledge

The insight Zumthor gains from his unique creative process is personal and hardly communicable: "Then I'm mostly surprised how similar the finished work is to the original sketch," he explains.[22] Elsewhere he sates: "I can't plan it. I only observe retrospectively, so in time the building becomes increasingly autonomous."[23]

From his project, Zumthor gains a better understanding of his own working method, which can by no means be fixed to a single style. Each project has a new approach. And with each project, he acquires greater skill and experience in the instruments and technique, both for the design and its implementation. Zumthor aims to discover, not invent.[24] Each project allows him to learn something new about his instruments, turning discovery into a project.

In this way, it is extremely difficult to imitate the work of Zumthor, because each new context means a new approach with new materials. Clearly such insight can neither be tested nor is it communicable. His approach is extremely personal and determined by doing. It is the work of a craftsman.

Zumthor also tellingly addresses the relationship between rational and irrational moments, whereby he stresses how ultimately the irrational, the "gut" wins out.[25]

Reflection

Although his work is very personal, Zumthor has always tried to describe and explain it in very short texts. Their plain, simple style reflects the straightforward nature of his projects.[26]

It is no surprise that Zumthor believes he has no knowledge of his own creative process, since it remains "unfathomable" to him.[27] However his texts allow him to understand the framework conditions better. The highlight to date in this process is presented in his book *Atmosphären*, published in 2006, where he best describes the content of his work using terms such as the book's title and its chapter headings, even though it remains personal.[28]

Zumthor is also constantly learning to observe the world better and investigates it in his search for images, which he successfully implements in his projects. In this sense, he is a phenomenologist rather than a theoretician. His comment on Goethe's journey through Italy seems fitting in this context: "When I hear stories about Johann Wolfgang von Goethe, it seems to me he set out on his famous journey through Italy not as a theoretician, but as a curious observer. He wanted to see and experience. He let things have an effect upon him. And that is exactly how I wish to continue to work. I initially wish to observe what I experience and feel: It is phenomenology, the study of observable facts."[29]

The actual research work lies in the observation, discovery and action on the one hand, but also in the implementation through the work in detail. The insight he gains is personal, strongly based on experience and helps him to better understand his own approach.

His spatial knowledge can be found in sketches, large-scale models and the deliberate qualities that flow out of the images into the space. It is also apparent in the poetic nature of his essays. They contain the continual quality of his spatial knowledge.

[26] "Peter Zumthor ist ein Phänomenologe seines Faches. Er beginnt mit jeder neuen Arbeit bei null. Das Ornamentale ist ihm suspekt – am Bau und im Diskurs. Er bemüht nicht Girlanden hochtrabender Theorie. Er baut. Und was er baut, das meint er auch." Meier 1992, p. 44
[27] Meier 1992, p. 47
[28] Zumthor 2006 (2)
[29] Zumthor 2006 (1), p. 59

Peter Zumthor: Therme Vals, 1996.
Interior photo. In: Zumthor 2007

Notes
Assessment of the case examples

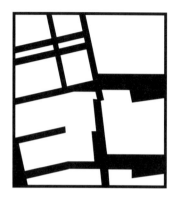

The example case studies presented here allow us to assess the personal background of each architect, the individual intentions arising from them and the use of specially developed instruments of architectural research and design for that purpose. They also provide information on the possible gain in cognition from the protagonists' individual creative architectural processes, the character of the spatial knowledge gained from it and its reception.

In an initial overview, it is apparent that personal background has a massive influence on the relevant architecture. In the diagrams, it is possible to see clear distinctions in the individual approaches. Above all, it is the starting point of each process – be it cognition, theory/reflection, implementation or the design – that reflects the different ways in which architecture is handled. Work with the diagram shows that a hierarchy of points and processes develops within the creative cycle. Not every architect touches on every node within this process with equal intensity and not every background flows into the same influence. Creative action develops around one or two focal points that are the subject of greater concentration.

Rossi's priority clearly lies in theory and only then in design, while for Eisenman, theory and design methods are equally important. Zumthor starts the process directly with the design, whereas Alexander operates via theory and Prouvé creates prototypes as a means of design, thereby going via implementation. So for Prouvé, the design process is reversed and his creativity takes a different course from the other examples studied here.

It also becomes apparent that the more one or two areas in the diagram are focused upon, the less influence the others have in the overall process. Eisenman is an extreme example, as he is simply not interested in the implementation of his work. By contrast, Zumthor reveals a balanced process in which the focal points lie in the design and implementation, as well as a great interest in reflection and theoretical examination.

The individual education of the architects or a personal interest in a different field apparently allows a more distanced perspective, making it easier to question architectural principles in an unbiased way. Zumthor for instance was trained as a furniture carpenter and worked in monumental preservation before founding his architectural office. Christopher Alexander studied mathematics before Architecture. Immediately after graduating in Architecture, Eisenman wrote a doctoral thesis on theoretical questions and was greatly interested in philosophy and literature, a passion he shared with Rossi, who was trained as an architect and intensively studied history and urban geography. Only Prouvé has a special status among our examples, since he was exclusively trained as a craftsman, but moved in a world dominated by architecture and art. They all share a perspective on architecture that is broadened by other fields. The situation of the protagonists leads them to question dominant conventions and methods and to continuously test and further develop their own actions in the sense of architectural research.

The instruments of the creative process are developed according to their weighting in the diagram – as well as the nature of their relationships, i.e. their connections. Both Eisenman and Alexander mainly work with diagrams they mainly draw from the context of natural sciences. Examples from art history also play a role for Eisenman – above all Colin Rowe, who formulated a new interpretation of diagrams. Very early on, Eisenman worked with computer models and was partially involved in developing the 3D software *FormZ*, which plays an appropriate role in his design work. By contrast, Rossi initially established drawings of urban plans as an analytical instrument, while self-developed "scientific" treatises complemented the creative process. Prouvé no longer placed craftsman's prototypes and industrial manufacturing techniques at the end of the design process, instead making them early steps in the work process, thereby giving them the role of an instrument. Zumthor developed many conventional architectural instruments further by varying the presentation of initial sketches or the scales of his

[1] Eisenman's work with diagrams is an example of this. In 1999 he dedicated a book to the subject, *Diagram Diaries*, which included a typological classification of diagrams and an overview of his entire work from the perspective of the relevant diagram.

[2] In his book *Content* (2004), Rem Koolhaas also records his urban planning strategies in the form of (fictitious) patents.

models to allow atmospheric qualities to be experienced at an early stage.

All the architects studied here actively seek instruments and methods and test them in an experimental way to achieve their intentions in architecture. They gain cognition by experimenting, which in turn leads to knowledge of one's own working methods.[1]

The question of the reception of the gained spatial knowledge goes hand in hand with the question of the instruments available to an architect for formulating his knowledge. Assuming that verbal communication is only possible to a limited extent, the study presents alternative solutions: Prouvé for instance uses patents as a good way of formulating his knowledge in the form of manufacturing processes.[2] In Eisenman's case, the knowledge is mainly presented using diagrams and theoretical texts, whereby the content of both levels, text and diagrammatic presentations, rarely overlap. Eisenman can rather be regarded as a founder of a poetic theory that is only indirectly communicated, using suggestion and theoretical constructs. His models, which sometimes distance themselves from the constructed building and represent additional project content, are further instruments for communicating knowledge. Such an example is the House X, which is now in the *Museum of Modern Art*. It was built in a way that it only appears "correct" from one position and thereby draws attention to the influence of architectural representation. Alexander mainly uses the form of mathematical textbooks to logically decode individual steps in a design process. Rossi mainly communicates his knowledge using highly suggestive drawings and montages, which simultaneously express his design methods. In a second communication instrument – his publications – Rossi for instance builds the *architecture of the city* on the basis of scientific treatises, while his own *Scientific Autobiography* plays on the impossibility of such a scientific quality, presenting it as a subjectively usable instrument. With Zumthor, oversized models are the main communicators of intended atmospheric properties. At the same time, he uses suggestive books such as *Atmospheres*, in which his projects are not shown themselves, and refers to the origins of his intentions by means of reference images.

Communicating the concrete form and range of spatial knowledge apparently requires an equally large field of experimentation,
as well as the development of methods of architectural creation.

Result
Summary and résumé of the project

[1] "Dabei geht es nicht darum, die Architektur in begrifflicher Schattenboxerei einem überdehnten Wissenschaftsbegriff unterzuordnen. Für die Wissenschaften geht es darum, die spezifische Produktionsform der Architektur ernst zu nehmen und möglicherweise daraus für eigene zeitgemässe Forschungsstrategien zu lernen." Schumacher 2001, p. 28

Is architecture research?

The result of this study clearly gives the overall creative architectural process a character of research. Architecture generates independent knowledge, which – like all knowledge resulting from research – is developed to understand things better. It distinguishes itself from other sciences in its nature and the way it can be assessed. While in traditional scientific fields, research can be assessed in terms of its ability to be comprehended and falsified, architectural research requires other criteria.

The knowledge generated through the architectural process is described here as spatial knowledge and unfolds in projects on and the implementation of space. The difficulty in defining architectural research lies in the discrepancy between the virtual impossibility of verbally communicating it and the necessary sustainability of the gained cognition. It is therefore clear that architecture is not a science and must instead be understood as one of many possible forms of knowledge. This perception seems to be slowly establishing itself, although only few studies have shed light on the specific nature of architectural knowledge.[1]

In this study, research in general was assessed in terms of its diversity, to perceive models that undermine the primacy of rational concepts of scientific research. It appears that new considerations stress aspects of action and experience, as well as regarding action to be strongly anchored in science. It is therefore possible to suggest that cognition and knowledge are only generated through action.

The case examples clearly show how spatial knowledge can be generated and communicated in an architectural process. An architect working through the cycle several times gains cognition on the process itself and the possibilities of implementing specific intentions, thereby achieving knowledge. This knowledge can be classified as research cognition if it is communicated to other architects and can be sustained by them. The communicability of architectural knowledge lies especially in the development of and reflection upon instruments and methods. This means that one requirement for research in architecture is to address one's own action, without being able to do so comprehensively using language. This in turn requires an architect's intention – although it cannot always be clearly expressed in words. Such an intention consists of wishing to spatially implement one's own ideas in architecture at all.

The model presented here suggests no generally applicable design, but assumes that every architect develops his own design method that is deliberately tuned towards his intentions. Architecture that pursues no intentions, that does not wish to change or improve anything, thereby failing to question and extend architecture itself and its instruments, does not carry out research, since it does not require it.

While the sustainability of the created knowledge was initially posited as a condition and described here as being achieved through method and instruments, we can now add that without a research intention in the creative process, only spatial knowledge is created. This will to research is apparent in the necessity of developing a personal set of tools, techniques and methods that provide support in achieving one's intentions.

All the architects studied here play an important role in the profession, not least because they researched and developed spatial knowledge that has had a sustained influence on other architects. If one takes reception as an indicator of significance, it is possible to conclude that quality in architecture is dependent on the existence of research and that the will to research is a precondition for good architecture – researching architecture.

Biscuits and Single Family Homes

Extracts from a discussion on aspects of science and knowledge in architecture

The participants in the discussion on January 26, 2009 were Michael Hampe, Professor of Philosophy in the Department of Human, Social and Political Sciences at the ETH Zurich and Reto Geiser, architect and curator of the Swiss Pavilion at the last Architecture Biennale in Venice, as well as the authors of this publication. The discussion reflects the status of the project at the time.

Tina Unruh: (...) A later part of the project will focus on the historical relationship between art and science in general and specifically in architecture. By highlighting individual moments in history, it will show how architects have been influenced by cultural historical paradigm shifts and how they reacted to them. Two forms of cognition – namely mythical, poetic knowledge, and rational knowledge – are focused upon including their differences. (...)

Michael Hampe: The question of *logos* and *mythos* as a point of departure for the history of knowledge should be supplemented by the growing significance of the term *action* in understanding knowledge. You hinted at this aspect in your introduction by referring to Ryle and Polanyi[1]. The Platonic idea that a *mythos* existed and science followed afterwards, which Plato called *logos*, basically does without taking forms of action into account. Neither mythologists nor those who create a *logos* act according to Plato. The mythologist tells an unorganised story and the scientist behaves like Euclid, who produced an organised logos by translating a specific method of combining *logoi* or words or however you want to call them. By 1880 at the latest, many philosophers were convinced that both were wrong representations, since neither *mythos* nor *logos* work the way Plato thought.
One can perhaps discern three historical waves that placed an emphasis on the term *action* in science. The first is Pragmatism, the

[1] Ryle 1969; Polanyi 1967

second is Erlangen Constructivism and the third is the discussion raised by Ian Hacking in *Representing and Intervening*.²

An example demonstrating the close relationship between practical experience and knowledge comes for the field of music. Mozart is reported to have entered a room and saw an open score on the table. Mozart immediately said the score was poor. He was unable to read it through, but gained an impression from an initial glance at the page. Here too, one could say that he worked so often with musical notes that he immediately combined and no longer noticed how quickly he went through a score. In other words, going through a score is only an explanation of something one sees at first glance. However one interprets that, it supports the idea that even abrupt cognition must have something to do with a background of action. Someone who had never made music would not have such intuition.

Artists – you talked about Aldo Rossi earlier – have their own form of action, which is difficult to communicate. You have to be there, one has to reproduce it. Regardless whether positions stress the aspect of logic or myth, action is part of both. That is the same in sciences. Why must people carry out experimental practises? They must learn particular forms of action. It leads us to the question of what experimentation actually is. Is experimentation the testing of a theory, attempting to test what I already know by means of an experiment? Or is it the performance of a theory? Naturally, some consider an experiment to be a performance which either succeeds or fails. For the first time, a physical theory becomes similar to the story the mythologist has in his head. Then he goes into the laboratory and tries to perform it, and sometimes the performance succeeds and sometimes it does not. A playwright like Ibsen has an idea of his characters, who work in one way or another. Then he writes a piece and attempts to perform the play in the theatre and it succeeds or it fails. Perhaps one can say the same for architecture: One has specific ideas how the building should be. And then one tries to build it and the implementation either succeeds or fails. In all three forms, the physical research process, conceiving a play and designing a building, there is a very strong correlation between implementing action and the interrelationships of ideas. I believe it is questionable to separate the interrelationship of ideas from a specific proficiency in techniques of action. And that is perhaps my final point: This is exactly where the idea of Nelson Goodman applies, that the creation of knowledge always has to do with the transformation of symbolic interrelationships. (...) He also describes how gained cognition never occurs *ex nihilo* and that the process always has a rhythm of action. Because I am capable of a certain type of action, I think in a certain way and react in a specific way. An artist learns how to handle colours and brushes from his master. He is therefore able to use a specific knowledge of action and can react to it. Such reaction to the knowledge of action leads to him gaining a different perspective, which is his own – combined with brushes and colours – and he attempts to implement this new perspective by painting in a way that has not been done before. (...)

Perhaps the same exists in architecture. Architects learn to create buildings in a specific way and sooner or later it becomes their second nature. They therefore have implicit knowledge of constructing in a specific way. Can they react to that? Do they react to this knowledge and seek a different perspective on how one can build? And do they continue to materialise that reaction? Some react to what they have learned. That creates new forms of action. One can also find the process in science: 'Now I'll apply geometry to a sphere rather than a flat surface.' ...

This entire process has to do with your question of how subjectivity and objectivity interact, since often, widespread knowledge is already collective knowledge; everyone applies geometry to the flat surface – like Euclid. And everyone paints like Leonardo da Vinci, everyone composes like Haydn. And suddenly someone starts to react. That is not *creatio ex nihilio*! Instead, he is reacting to what he can already do extremely well. I think the relationship between subjectivity and objectivity is the reaction of individuals to the collective. If something is collective, it is objective and an individual reacts to it. His reaction is initially subjective, but if it succeeds and itself creates a collective that takes over his way of working, a new objectivity is created, since it has created a collective that says one has to do things that way... (...)

3 The authors would now express this in
a more differentiated way. However the
discussion reflects the status of the project
at the time.

Reto Geiser: I have a fundamental question. (...) You chose the term *architectural research* and imply that first a scientific basis is developed and then design begins in a chronologically staggered way.[3] This would lead to the supposition that the design itself is not suitable as a research instrument. You speak of architectural research, rather than explicitly design research. What is your position towards the fact that architecture itself is a field that is not limited to its own boundaries and is instead primarily supported by other fields? Research in the fields of Chemistry and Physics is carried out in architectural faculties. The results are then applied to practice and therefore the design. (...) The opposing question would be how can Design professors research? A majority of people working there have non-scientific educations. So the question is what kind of 'research' is being carried out? (...) As the discussion at the Biennale showed, there is debate on this aspect in many universities, both in Switzerland and abroad. It seems discussion on the subject is far from over. I can well remember how one Design professor said that as soon as he drew a line, that was research. I myself find that rather problematic. But is the inference true that a scientific element must first be established before one can integrate research into the design?

Tina Unruh: Such statements motivated us to work on this project. (...) In an ideal sense, architecture cannot be scientific since it cannot be falsified. For example if we take a competition with 100 entries and the jury awards the first prize to one design, presumably no jury would say that the other 99 designs are wrong and only the winner is right. Architecture undergoes the level of design, in which complete traceability no longer exists.

Andri Gerber: Unless one defines research differently.

Tina Unruh: That would be an alternative.

Andri Gerber: Or you could say that in architecture, design is analogous with research, but that kind of research is not scientific. But one would need to quantify it in that case. How would that be done?

Reto Geiser: (...) Let us take an example from a different field, in which its scientific nature is hardly questioned: *Artificial Intelligence*, as for instance taught by Rolf Pfeifer at Zurich University. The way research is carried out in this field is very similar to work known at the ETH Studio Basel[4] or the Harvard *Project on the City*.[5] It is a very playful, intuitive approach in which non-rational processes clearly play a part. Pfeifer calls it "Understanding by Design", while other institutions call it "Design Research" or "Research by Design". The aim is to use a creative, not necessarily hundred percent rational, approach to work on something, to reflect upon it and analyse it, thereby developing it further. The way in which work is done in such laboratories would not function at all if it had to be started by exclusively theoretical, scientific means. It is the parallel exchange between theory and practice that leads to the result. I found it interesting that a design approach can also be found in other fields in which scientific precision is never questioned.

Michael Hampe: I believe the relationship between play and method is very significant. Saying that research is always methodical only means there is always a specific form of approach. I can communicate this form of approach and others must follow it if they wish to participate in the research process. If one does not wish to use this approach, one is not permitted to participate in the research, since the action would be unmethodical.

In science, the pressure to adhere to tried and trusted methods is relatively high, even though significant innovation must occur at the same time. In art, this relationship between trusted methods and innovation is different and the pressure of innovation is much greater. Attention is paid to adhering to trusted methods and in art the term that is analogous to method is style. There are trusted styles. But it is boring and imitative to merely continue a style. It is expected from almost every individual in art to react to an existing style and create a new one. But it is only expected of exceptional mathematicians and physicists to create a new method in Physics or Mathematics.

If one makes a stark distinction and says this is art and this is science, and that art is unmethodical and science is methodical, the dis-

[4] Diener, R., Herzog, J., Meili, M., Meuron, P. de, Schmid, C. (Hg.), *Die Schweiz – ein städtebauliches Porträt*, Basel: Birkhäuser, 2006

[5] Koolhaas, Rem, *Harvard Design School, Project on the city*, Cologne: Taschen, 2001

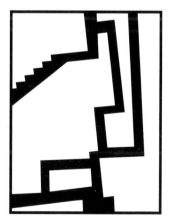

tinction disappears in certain areas. It disappears where science is innovative, for instance in researching super string theory in Physics or chaos studies and set theory. The people that initiated them were initially considered odd, almost as artists, who wish to create something completely new. Then they established themselves and a new method developed. There are probably imitators in art that merely continue a specific style and always build, paint and write poetry according to the same standard method. They are quasi-scientists without any new ideas, but they do something that is tried and trusted and may still work. In a community that considers innovation to be very important, they are not highly regarded. But a scientist who is not especially innovative, but is exceptional in continuing existing methods further, is likely to find recognition because people say not everyone can be like Einstein or Planck. But every architect must somehow be well known, a Koolhaas. So perhaps the question of what is research and what is art can be answered from the different emphasis of innovative pressure in the different communities? In more artistically oriented collectives, the pressure of innovation is much greater than in scientific collectives, where the pressure of method is much greater.

Andri Gerber: One question we have not yet answered is that of personal union: What is the relationship between the researcher and the designer? Must it be the same person that researches and then applies the cognition gained from it to the design or can one assume that someone can use new cognition by other researchers for their own purposes? The persons we wish to study basically carried out their own research, like Aldo Rossi, or they constructed their own research in a way that let them use it for their design, like Christopher Alexander, who was also a mathematician.

Reto Geiser: That is a good question, which I also wanted to pick up on: In most architectural schools, there are professors of Design and professors that teach history and theory. There is hardly any overlap and that means it is relatively difficult to bridge the gap between theoretical, historical themes and design teaching. At the University of Michigan, I taught both the design class and the foundation course – Design Fundamentals – which is based on theory and history. Many of my students attended both courses. So there were thematic overlaps and I discovered that a close connection between theory and practice can be very fruitful. The model of a personal union of the theoretician and designer can be found in many Anglo-American universities.

Michael Hampe: The idea of sustainability could play a role. In architectural history, as in cultural history, a distinction is made between what is sustainable and what is not sustainable. Something's sustainability is quite a good assessment criterion – and that applies both to methods and styles. If someone says, 'I have a new idea, I'm now going to do pictures like this,' and he can't say how he has produced the pictures, it may be an inability to step away from oneself and talk about it. But if he can produce a large number of pictures in this way and he moves into his blue phase and his name is Picasso, then you realise that something is sustainable – even if he can't provide any information on it. It becomes a way of painting pictures. By now there is an opposing movement in science: Comby wrote 4 volumes entitled *Styles of reasoning*, in which the term style is applied to the sciences. In the history of science, what used to be called method was then called style. There was a style of calculating in the 14th Century and there was a style of experimenting with Archimedes, which Galileo picked up on. That means there was a sustainable form of carrying out experiments or a sustainable form of calculating. This perspective brings the terms style and method very close together and leads to an autonomous assessment criterion. If I can sustain something, it has substance, regardless whether I can explain it or not. And if another person can't sustain it, we're talking about a bluff. If a picture appears and one doesn't know whether it is a Picasso or not, it's a criterion suggesting that someone else could paint like Picasso – or calculate like Euclid. If one argued scientifically, one could say there is only one method of production.

Andri Gerber: The question is whether it is a method...

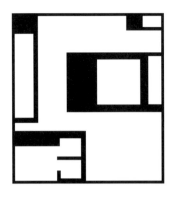

Michael Hampe: ...or a style.

Andri Gerber: Or only one style. In the case of Aldo Rossi, everyone painted that way at his time. They all had that specific technique, it looked like Rossi...

Dieter Geissbühler: Yes, they even all used the same paper. (...)

Reto Geiser: The most difficult question is how one moves from analysis to design. Carrying out both research and design simultaneously in a design studio is a demanding task. The ETH Studio Basel limited itself to research – at least during the early phase of the Switzerland project[6] – at a time when I was studying at the institute. At a later date, suggestive projects were also conceived to illustrate the project theses, but were not developed into comprehensive architectural designs. I had similar experiences in Michigan, where I worked together with students on fringe situations within the city of Detroit. There too, the transformation from analysis to the project was the greatest challenge. It was essential for the discussions with the authorities and the public to implement the abstract cognition derived from the analysis into a thesis project. I am generally assuming that a project is included in design research. In the 'Städtebauliche Portrait der Schweiz' for instance, a large synthesised map was developed that divided Switzerland into different zones and demonstrated potential for future urban development. The map is an example of merging scientific research with a conceptual, intuitive approach. The maps are based on statistical information such as commuter flows and population densities, but were then supplemented by unquantifiable knowledge that was gained from the specific observation of locations by means of inspections and photographic documentation. In this way, boundaries were drawn that were neither scientifically definable nor arbitrary. I believe something was thereby created that is relevant and could only be produced by such a design research group.

[6] Diener, R., Herzog, J., Meili, M., Meuron, P. de, Schmid, C. (Ed.), *Die Schweiz – ein städtebauliches Porträt*, Basel: Birkhäuser, 2006

Tina Unruh: It is striking that architectural schools carrying out 'research in or on teaching' generally refer to their urban planning seminars. It seems that urban planning is well suited to allow methodical approaches to flow into it and thereby gain a certain scientific level. I presume that has to do with the fact that urban planning is strongly rooted in analysis. It requires large-scale urban planning analysis, for which different forms of knowledge can be used – ranging from sociology to statistics. (...)

Reto Geiser: The distinction between *urban planning* and *planning* or *urban design* is a cultural question. In the USA, there was initially only *urban planning*, as *urban design* was only introduced as a separate field by Josep Lluís Sert at Harvard University in the late 1950s. What goes without saying today did not even exist. The field of *urban design* stemmed from the idea that not only administrators and technicians work on the city, but the designing architect can also contribute. In the context of Switzerland, where regional planning was introduced in the late fifties, there was no strict distinction between architecture, urban planning and planning. (...)

Tina Unruh: Our initial question is whether architecture is a scientific field. Most architects do not regard their field as such. In the case of urban planning, an automatic scientific assumption is present, since other fields – which are also regarded as scientific – flow into it. But in principle, analysis precedes every design. (...) And there are other architects who integrate a catalogue of endless questions into the process. So we must detach ourselves a little from urban planning by making analysis and its extradisciplinary parameters more traceable. The 'common design' is much more interesting for our question, since the criteria the analysis takes into account and the way in which knowledge is generated are not discussed precisely. So we return to the initial question by Andri Gerber, which we have not yet answered: Must the designing architect also carry out research and gain knowledge according to scientific standards? Or is it unnecessary and the architect can draw from general knowledge?

Andri Gerber: The question that goes with it is how specifically research must already refer to the design. Or in other words, to what extent can research be coincidental, allowing the architect to simply use something which he did not necessarily think would change the design?

Tina Unruh: It is the question of reverberation and self-consciousness. Was knowledge explicitly sought before the design process or can the knowledge be experiences that I involuntarily or unconsciously integrate into it?

Andri Gerber: Our task of establishing parameters for architectural research is almost impossible, since the way in which research is integrated into the architectural process might be one which was not foreseen by the research.

Tina Unruh: That is the great problem…

Andri Gerber: The architects we intend to look at in case studies have all carried out underlying research or referred to existing research that interested them. (…) Christopher Alexander for instance does not only seek content in but also methodical aspects of a mathematical basis. He makes a connection between content and method. Perhaps one should study that methodical aspect and make it available. The question would then be whether the content continues to follow or whether it becomes merely a question of style.

Michael Hampe: Have you investigated the parallel with medicine? The field is in a similar situation. There are pre-clinical and clinical studies. The first part of the study is pre-clinical, which is theoretical, while the second part of the study is diagnostic, pathological, where healing occurs and clinical profiles are demonstrated. The precondition is that one must first gain cognition through human biological research and then react in a diagnostic and therapeutic way. So research is a precondition of therapy. That is very similar to what you presented in urban planning: Analysis plays the role of research and design is analogous with application in the natural sciences.

Tina Unruh: ... So it is the application of knowledge that I have consciously gained in advance.

Andri Gerber: Although architectural studies are based on design from the very beginning. The other subjects complement it, but design is central from the outset.

Reto Geiser: What I consider dangerous is when one suggests that architecture can solve problems... The idea of solving problems with a design is closely connected to the question of external reception, but also the self-perception of the architects. Clearly one can address problems with a design, but especially if we are discussing the level of urban planning, the question arises of what one can actually solve. Many processes are too complex and intricate for one person alone to control.

Michael Hampe: I did not mean to define medicine as analogous with architecture. It was instead intended as a recommendation for the organisation of architectural presentation.

Andri Gerber: ... or rather how it is considered.

Michael Hampe: Until the end of the 19ᵗʰ Century, doctors were people who practised something like an art – the art of healing. Then medicine become scientific and an idea developed that one must first be scientifically trained. Since 1860, it has been impossible to become a doctor without the precondition of scientific knowledge. Today there is a kind of backlash: People say we need a general practitioner again who commands his art and does not practise apparatus medicine, does not constantly read scientific journals and reacts to the individual. *De facto*, exactly the opposite happens in a hospital: You are shoved in, tissue samples are sent to the pathologist, blood samples go to the laboratory etc. and then the feedback from there dictates the therapy. This development is hardly questioned by the general public or in science magazines. [...] That situation is perhaps analogous to architecture. There is not such a strong scientific tendency, but there is a pressure to state what kind of research is being carried out. That is a similar phenomenon. If a great deal of knowledge flows in, a research process must also control how the knowledge is integrated. It is similar to the general practitioner who only briefly talks to someone, knocks him on the chest and already believes he knows the patient's problem. There is great scepticism towards the implied experience, which can be demonstrated. (...)

Andri Gerber: In our project, we should not reduce architecture to a method, which is a danger that comes with the field of science. We do not believe one can reduce everything to a system. It is the particular mixture that Reto Geiser discussed that characterises architecture. Whether one can unravel it at all or not and whether it would thereby become too scientific...

Michael Hampe: But especially in urban planning, I have the impression, without knowing exactly, that there are strong analogies with areas of medicine that work on epidemics. The spread of disease is on the one hand highly scientific, with statistics and enormous studies that are, scientifically speaking, very complex. On the other hand, the spread of disease always has to do with a lifestyle. If people in western Europe have diabetes, it is because they always eat so many biscuits. Naturally epidemiologists have no influence on that. They can only observe the fact, but they are unable to therapeutically change people's lifestyles. I have a feeling that when people talk about cities, for instance when Lampugnani[7] says, the spread of single family homes is destroying the landscape, then a lifestyle is also being criticised. A diagnosis is made, a lifestyle is criticised, but as an individual architect it is impossible to act against it. Like the epidemiologist who cannot forbid people to eat biscuits, the urban planner cannot ban single family homes. It is a similar constellation, although ecological and health matters differ, but I see the similarity between the two fields there.

[7] "Es wird eng. Jeder will ein eigenes Haus, doch viele Häuser machen noch kein Dorf. Was Raumplaner Weisslingen empfehlen." Interview mit Vittorio Magnago Lampugnani, NZZ Folio. Mai 2007. p. 18–23

Andri Gerber: What you say is interesting. Urban planning was very late to develop as a field in its own right. Doctors in Manchester and Liverpool were the first to carry out such studies. So there are many biological metaphors. So the first investigations of cities were also made from a medical perspective.

Reto Geiser: I think it is very good that you are conducting this project and taking a really in-depth look at the subject. The pressure for research came from Bologna. I think some things happen less consciously at the two ETHs, since research has been going on around us for a long time. But that does not mean that – with the exception of human scientists and construction physicists – a clear idea of research exists in the Department of Architecture, especially with respect to the question of design. That was also the reason why I wanted to organise the symposia in connection with the exhibition here in Switzerland.[8] It was not because I had the feeling that the subject would thereby be resolved, but because it could perhaps initiate a fruitful discussion. I think it is great that you are also addressing that and I found the discussion very stimulating.

[8] www.designexplorations.org

Bibliography

Alexander, Christopher/Neis, Hajo/Anninou, Artemis/King, Ingrid: *A new theory of urban design*. New York: Oxford University Press, 1987

Alexander, Christopher: *The Timeless Way of Building*. New York: Oxford University Press, 1979

Alexander, Christopher/Ishikawa, Sara/Silverstein, Murray: *A Pattern Language, Towns – Buildings – Construction*. New York: Oxford University Press, 1977

Alexander, Christopher: *The Oregon Experiment*. New York: Oxford University Press, 1975

Alexander, Christopher: *Notes on the synthesis of Form*. Cambridge: Harvard University Press, 1964

Alexander, Christopher/Manheim, Marvin L.: *Hidecs 2: A computer Program for the hierarchical Decomposition of a set which has an associated linear graph*. Cambridge MA: Departement of Civil Engineering, M.I.T., Publication No. 160, June 1962

Aristoteles: *Nikomachische Ethik*. German translation and epilogue by Franz Dirtmeier, Notes by Ernst A. Schmidt, 2003

Archieri, Jean-François: *Prouvé: Cours du CNAM 1957–1970 Essai de reconstitution du cours à partir des archives Jean Prouvé*. Liège: Mardaga, 1990

Arnold, Madeleine: *Les Modèles chez Alexander, Approche critique du Pattern Language*. Centre d'études de recherches architecturales, Ecole nationale supérieure des beaux arts, 1977

Balzert, H./Schäfer, C./Schröder, M./Kern, U.: *Wissenschaftliches Arbeiten, Wissenschaft, Quellen, Artefakte, Organisation, Präsentation*. Herdecke/Witten: W3L-Verlag, 2008

Bartels, Andreas/Stöckler, Manfred (Ed.): *Wissenschaftstheorie*. Paderborn: Mentis, 2007

Becker, Annette et al (Ed.): *Aldo Rossi – Die suche nach dem Glück: Frühe Zeichnungen und Entwürfe*. München: Prestel, 2003.

Berg, Anne Marie/Eikeland, Olav (Ed.): *Action Research*. Frankfurt am Main: Peter Lang, 2008. S. 7–8

Beyer, Andreas/Lohoff, Markus (Ed.): *Bild und Erkenntnis, Formen und Funktionen des Bildes in Wissenschaft und Technik*. München: Deutscher Kunstverlag, 2005

"Bilder befragen, Interview mit Peter Zumthor". In: *Daidalos* 68, Juni 1998. p. 90–101

Böhme, Gernot: *Alternativen der Wissenschaft*. Frankfurt am Main: Suhrkamp Verlag, 1980

Bonsiepe, Gui: "Von der Praxisorientierung zur Erkenntnisorientierung oder: Die Dialektik von Entwerfen und Entwurfsforschung", *Erstes Design Forschungssysmposium*. HGK Basel, Swissdesignnetwork, 2004. p. 15–21

Boudon, Philippe: *Der architektonische Raum, Über das Verhältnis von Bauen und Erkennen* [1971]. Aus dem Französischen von Marianne Uhl. Berlin: Birkhäuser Verlag, 1991

Broadbent, Geoffrey/Ward, Anthony (Ed.): *Design Methods in Architecture*, Architectural Association Paper Number 4. London: Lund Humphires. p. 19–26

Brockhaus, Die Enzyklopädie, 20., überarbeitete und aktualisierte Auflage, 6. Band. DUD-EV, 1996

Camartin, Iso: "Die Geisteswissenschaften, Relikt der Vergangenheit oder Rezept für die Zukunft?". In: Schweizerische Hochschulkonferenz (Ed.), *Wissenschaft und Forschung*, Beiheft 50, 1991. p. 43–54

Chermayeff, Serge/Alexander, Christopher: *Community and Privacy, Toward a New Architecture of Humanism* [1963]. Armondsworth: Penguin Books, 1965

Ciorra, Pippo: *Peter Eisenman: opere e progetti*, con un saggio di Giorgio Ciucci. Milano: Electa, 1993

"Conversation with Peter Eisenman". In: Bédard, Jean-François (Ed.), *Cities of Artificial Excavation*, The Work of Peter Eisenman, 1978–1988. Montréal: Centre Canadien d'Architecture, Rizzoli International Publication, 1994. p. 118–129

Cross, Nigel: *Designerly Ways of Knowing*. London: Springer, 2006

Cross, Nigel: "Design Method and scientific method". In: Robin, Jacques/Powell, James A (Ed.): *Design: Science: Method, Proceedings of the 1980 Design Research Society Conference*. Surrey: Westbury House, 1980. p. 15–21

Cross, Nigel: "Design and Research, Developing a Discipline". In: *Drawing new Territories*, Swiss Design Network, 2006. p. 26

De Bruyn, Gerd: *Die enzyklopädische Architektur*. Bielefeld: transcript Verlag, 2008

Diemer, Alwin (Ed.), *Konzeption und Begriff der Forschung in den Wissenschaften des 19. Jahrhunderts*. Meisenheim am Glan: Verlag Anton Hain, 1978

Dreyfus, J.: "Christopher Alexander ou le mythe de la création scientifique". In: La vie urbaine, no. 2, 1971. p. 140–148

Dombois, Florian: "Das Design am Übergang von Naturwissenschaftlicher und künstlerischer Forschung". In: *Forschungslandschaften im Umfeld des Designs*, Swiss Design Network, Zweites Design Forschungssymposium, Swiss Design Network, 2005. p. 45

Eisenman, Peter: *Diagram Diaries*. London: Thames & Hudson, 1999

Eisenman, Peter: "Unfolding Events: Frankfurt Rebstock and the Possibility of a New Urbanism" [1991]. In: *Re:working Eisenman*. London: The Academy Group, 1993. p. 58–61

Eisenman, Peter: "Blue Line Text". In: Architectural Design, Nr. 7/8, Vol. 58, 1988. p. 6–9

Eisenman, Peter: "Misreading Peter Eisenman". In: Eisenman, Peter, *Petereisenmanhousesofcards*. New York: Oxford University Press, 1987. p. 167–186

Eisenman, Peter: "A review of Allison and Peter Smithson's Ordinariness and Light". In: Architectural Forum, May 1971 (C). p. 76–80

"Entwurfsmuster". In: Arch+ Nr. 189, Oktober 2008

Feyerabend, Paul/Thomas, Christian (Hg.): *Kunst und Wissenschaft*. Zürich: Verlag der Fachvereine, 1984.

Gamma, Erich et al (Ed.): *Entwurfsmuster* [1995]. Bonn: Addison-Wesley, 2004

Gibbons, Michael, et al: *The new production of knowledge. The dynamics of science and research in contemporary societies*. London: Sage, 1994

Giddens, Anthony: *Die Konstitution der Gesellschaft: Grundzüge einer Theorie der Strukturierung*, [1984], 3. Auflage. Frankfurt: Campus Verlag, 1997

Glanville, Ranulph: "Design and Mentation: Piaget's constant objects 2". In: A Design Culture Journal, 2005

Glanville, Ranulph: "Re-searching Design and Designing Research". In: Design Issues, vol. 13, no 2, 1999

Grabow, Stephen/Alexander, Christopher: *The Search for a new Paradigm in Architecture*. Stocksfield: Oriel Press, 1983

Guidot, Raimond: *Jean Prouvé "constructeur"*. Katalog zur Ausstellung 24. Okt. 1990–28. Januar 1991 im Rahmen des Renzo Piano Building Workshops in der Galerie des CCI. Paris: Centre national d'arte et de culture George Pompidou, 1990

Hacking, Ian: *Representing and Intervening, Introductory topics in the philosophy of natural science*. Cambridge: Cambridge University Press, 1983

Hays, Michael (Ed.): *Architecture theory since 1968*. Cambridge MA: MIT Press, 1998

Heymann, Matthias: *"Kunst" und Wissenschaft in der Technik des 20. Jahrhunderts, Zur Geschichte der Konstruktionswissenschaft*. Zürich: Chronos Verlag, 2005

Jacobson, Max: "Max Jacobson Interviews Christopher Alexander". In: Architectural Design, no. 768, 1971. p. 768

Jaeger, Friedrich: *Enzyklopädie der Neuzeit*. Stuttgart/Weimar: Verlag J. B. Metzler, 2005

Kämpf-Jansen, Helga: *Ästhetische Forschung, Wege durch Alltag, Kunst und Wissenschaft*. Köln: Salon Verlag, 2001

Keller, Sean: "System Aesthetics, or How Cambridge Solved Architecture". In: Anstey, Tim/Grillner, Katja/Hughes, Rolf (Ed.): *Architecture and Autorship*. London: Black Dog Publishing, 2007. p. 156–163

Kluge, Friedrich: *Etymologisches Wörterbuch*. Berlin: de Gruyter, 1989

"Kommentare zur Zürcher Lehrtätigkeit von Aldo Rossi". In: Werk, Bauen + Wohnen Nr. 12, 1997

Kuhn, Thomas: *Die Struktur wissenschaftlicher Revolutionen* [1962]. Frankfurt am Main: Suhrkamp, 1991

"La régression californienne ou la réification du mythe, Christopher Alexander, une Conférence". In: AMC 38, 1976. p. 76–77

Latour, Alessandra/Vinciarelli, Lauretta: "Entretien avec Peter Eisenman, Propos recueillis à New York le 11 octobre 1976". In: Architecture Mouvement Continuité, Nr. 41, 1977. p. 56–62

Latour, Bruno: *La science en action, Introduction à la sociologie des sciences* [1987]. Paris: Gallimard, 1995. p. 50

Lévi-Strauss, Claude: *Das wilde Denken*, 10. Auflage. Frankfurt am Main: Suhrkamp, 1997

Lewin, Kurt: *Die Lösung sozialer Konflikte* [1948]. Bad Nauheim: Christian Verlag, 1968

Mandl, Heinz/Gerstenmaier, Jochen (Ed.): Die Kluft zwischen Wissen und Handeln. Göttingen: Hogrefe, 2000

Meier, Marco: "Peter Zumthor: Architektur der Gelassenheit". In: Du, Heft Nr. 5, Mai 1992. p. 47–48

Mittelstrass, Jürgen (Ed.): *Enzyklopädie Philosophie und Wissenschafts-theorie*, Band 2: C-F, 2., neubearbeitete und wesentlich ergänzte Ausgabe. Stuttgart, Weimar: Verlag J. B. Metzler, 1980–1996

Moore, Gary T. (Ed.), *Emerging Methods in Environmental Design and Planning*, Proceedings of The Design Methods Group, First International Conference, Cambridge Massachusetts, June 1968. Cambridge MA: MIT Press, 1970.

Moravánszky Ákos/Fischer Ole W.: *Precisions, Architektur zwischen Wissen-schaft und Kunst*. Berlin: Jovis Verlag, 2008

Moravánszky Ákos: *ETH Zürich Seminar (051-0236-07), Architekturtheorie Aldo Rossi, Poetischer Rationalismus*. Sommersemester 2007

Peters, Nils: *Jean Prouvé 1901–1984. Die Dynamik der Schöpfung*. Köln: Taschen Verlag, 2006

Pfäffli, Brigitta K.: *Lehren an Hochschulen*. Bern: Haupt, 2005

Peirce, Charles Sanders: "5.172", *Collected papers of Charles Sanders Peirce, Volume V, Pragmatism and Pragmaticism and Volume VI, Scientific Metaphysics*. Cambridge MA: The Belknap Press of University Harvard University Press, 1974–1979. p. 105–107

Polany, Michael: *The Taut Dimension*. London: Routledge, 1967

Prouvé, Jean/Huber, Benedikt/Steinegger, Jean-Claude (Ed.): *Jean Prouvé*. Zürich: Verlag für Architektur Artemis, 1971

Purini, Franco: "A proposito degli scritti di Peter Eisenman, Ed infine un classico". In: Casabella, Nr. 541, Dicembre 1987, p. 36–37

Rheinberger, Hans-Jörg/Hagner, Michael/Wahrig-Schmidt, Bettina (Hg.): *Räume des Wissens, Repräsentation, Codierung, Spur*. Berlin: Akademie Verlag, 1997.

Rossi, Aldo: *L'Architettura della città*, Padua 1966, Englische Ausgabe 1982, Deutsche Ausgabe 1973

Rossi, Aldo: *Wissenschaftliche Selbstbiographie*. Bern: Verlag Gachnang & Springer AG, Bern 1988

Rossi, Aldo: *The Architecture of the City*. Cambridge MA: Oppositions Books, The Institute for Architecture and Urban Studies and The Massachusetts Institute of Technology, 1982

Russell, Bertrand: *The Problems of Philosophy* [1912]. Oxford: Oxford University Press, 1998

Ryle, Gilbert: *Der Begriff des Geistes*. Stuttgart: Philipp Reclam Jun., 1969

Sack, Manfred: "Über Peter Zumthors Art zu entwerfen, also zu denken". In: Zumthor, Peter: *Drei Konzepte*. Luzern: Edition Architekturgalerie, 1997. p. 69–76

Schumacher, Christina: "Dogged by the model of science, Ist Architektur Wissenschaft?". In: tec 21, 13/2001. p. 25–28

Schwarz, Ulrich: *Peter Eisenman, Aura und Exzess, Zur Überwindung der Metaphysik der Architektur*. Wien: Passagen Verlag, 1995

Seabrook, John: "The David Lynch of Architecture". In: Vanity Fair, January 1991. p. 74–79

Second EAAE-ENHSA Sub-network Workshop on Architectural Theory, 2008

Sennett, Richard: *Handwerk*, Aus dem Amerikanischen von Michael Bischoff. Berlin: Berlin Verlag, 2008

Sequin Jousse Galerie-Galerie Enrico Navarra (Hg.): *Jean Prouvé*, Paris, 1998

Stringer, Ernest T.: *Action Research*. Newbury Park CA: Sage Publications, 2007

Sulzer, Peter/Sulzer-Kleinemeier, E.: *Jean Prouvé. The complete Works 1917–1933 (1923–1933)*. Berlin: Wasmuth Verlag, 1995

Teyssot Georges: "Marginal comments on the debate between Alexander and Eisenman". In: Lotus International 40, 1983/IV. p. 69–73

Vegesack, Alexander von (Ed.): *Jean Prouvé, Die Poetik des technischen Objekts*, Katalog zur Ausstellung. Weil am Rhein: Vitra Design Museum, 2006

Wallner, Fritz G./Agnese, Barnara (Ed.): *Von der Einheit des Wissens zur Vielfalt der Wissensformen*. Wien: Wilhelm Braumüller, 1997

Zumthor, Peter: *Therme Vals*. Zürich: Scheidegger & Spiess, 2007

Zumthor, Peter: "Körper und Bild". In: *Zwischen Bild und Realität/Ralf Konersmann/Peter Noever/Peter Zumthor*. Zürich: GTA Verlag, 2006. (1) p. 58–75

Zumthor, Peter: *Atmosphären, architektonische Umgebungen, die Dinge um mich herum*. Basel: Birkhäuser, 2006 (2)

Zumthor, Peter: *Drei Konzepte, Thermalbad Vals, Kunsthaus Bregenz, «Topographie des Terrors» Berlin*. Luzern: Edition Architekturgalerie, 1997

"Das spezifische Gewicht der Architektur, '...begeistert vom Körper', Ein Gespräch mit Peter Zumthor". In: Archithese Nr. 5, September-Oktober, 1996. p. 28–33

Zumthor, Peter: "Der harte Kern der Schönheit". In: Du, Heft Nr. 5, Mai 1992. p. 68–72

Laboratorium

Laboratorium: An environment of study in which to reflect, but above all to work and experiment. It is not just for testing, but also for pooling ideas and theories, in brief – a place of research. Because *laborare* not only means "to work", but also "to make an effort" and is therefore an activity with an open end and related to research.

Edited by: Hochschule Luzern – Technik & Architektur; Competence Centre Material, Structure & Energy in Architecture, Tina Unruh

Volume 1: Climate as a Design Factor
Contributions: Roman Brunner, Christian Hönger, Urs-Peter Menti, Christoph Wieser

This volume studies the climate as a design factor and examines its influence on energy and design consequences. Instead of an abstract, technical perspective, the approach is illustrative and spatial, thereby consciously stimulating the search for inspirational solutions.

112 pages, 17×22 cm, German (partly in English)
ISBN 978-3-03761-010-7

Quart Verlag GmbH, Heinz Wirz
CH-6006 Luzern
books@quart.ch, www.quart.ch

Kompetenzzentrum Material, Struktur & Energie in Architektur
Hochschule Luzern – Technik & Architektur
http://www.hslu.ch/technik-architektur